Kirsty Budding is a playwright based in Canberra, Australia. She holds degrees in Literature and History from the Australian National University. Kirsty runs a theatre company specialising in drama education and youth theatre. Her first book, *Paper Cuts: Comedic and Satirical Monologues for Audition or Performance* won the 2018 ACT Writing and Publishing Award for Fiction. This is her second book.

THE 100

THE 100

New and Classic Monologues for
Children & Young Adults

KIRSTY BUDDING

First published 2019 by
Budding Theatre
Canberra ACT, Australia
www.buddingtheatre.com

Cover design by Sengsavane Chounramany (www.sengsavane.wordpress.com).
Interior Photography by Greg Gould

ISBN: 978-0-6487421-0-4

A catalogue record for this
book is available from the
National Library of Australia

For my Family

&

Zane

Acknowledgement

The playwright would like to gratefully acknowledge the children and young adults who first performed these monologues at the launch of 'The 100' in Canberra, Australia on December 14th, 2019.

Arthur Cole (6)
Vincent Hemmings (6)
Caitlin Hunt (6)
Rosie Welling (6)
Crystelle Cox (8)
Lincoln Newell (8)
Lilia Wilson (8)
Sophie Kelly (9)
Angeline Mengel (9)
Harper Scott (9)
Madison Willmott (9)
Edith Baggoley (10)
Fraser Gardiner (10)
Toby Gosling-Dunlop (10)
Tayla Holt (11)
Taylor Lloyd (10)
Eleanor Graham (11)
Charlotte Hunt (11)
Sophie McConnell (11)
Addison Prentice (11)
Erin Stiles (11)
Ella Jalkanen (12)
Amy Mahoney (12)
Caitlin McMillan (12)
Lara Buchanan (13)
Sylvia Hemmings (13)
Jessica Kelly (13)
Hannah McConnell (13)
Alex Peek (13)
Indigo Scott (13)
Sam Welling (13)
Charleigh Byrne (14)
Elodie Khan (14)
Eva Meffert (14)
Vivien Murray (14)
Sara Patil (14)
Callum White (14)
Abigail Boddington (15)
Rosie Brady (15)
Féy Etherington (15)
Aimee Halley (15)
Lachlan Herring (15)
Lexie Hollow (15)
Breanna Kelly (15)
Lily Mae Harrison (15)
Bridie McArthur (15)
Mia Newman (15)
Saffron Murrells (15)
Isabel Pereira (15)
Francesca Stuparich (15)
Lily Welling (15)
Adele Beaumont (16)
Olivia Boddington (16)
Jessica Dickie (16)
Maxwell Etherington (16)
Quinn Goodwin (16)
Ella Buckley (17)
Sarah Jackson (17)
Hannah Ward (17)
Gabriella Van Runt (17)
Robert Wearden (17)
Remus Douglas (18)
Jack Morton (19)
Matilda Saddington (19)
Caitlin Addinell (19)
Bertram O'Brien (20)

Contents

Drama

Teen Life

Classic Characters from Literature

Historical Figures

Simply Shakespeare

Introduction from the playwright

In developing monologues for 'The 100', I drew inspiration from the children and young people I work with through my theatre company, responding to the characters, situations and challenges they wanted to explore. This has resulted in a collection that caters to the imaginations of actors ages five to nineteen, from a child scared of monsters under the bed, to a young adult moments from their twentieth birthday.

Some are set in reality, some are fantastical, some are funny, some are sad, some are inspired by myth and legend, some are about everyday pressures like school, exams and social media, some are based on historical figures, and some are adaptations of classic characters from literature. I have also included a Simply Shakespeare section for performers aspiring to study acting beyond school, as a Shakespearean monologue is an audition requirement for most drama schools.

In each section, the monologues range in length and complexity, providing challenges for performers of different ages and experience levels. My hope is that it can provide a useful resource for siblings of different ages, or be used across year groups in school contexts. Time lengths range from thirty seconds for very young children to over five minutes for older performers. I recommend performers always time themselves when preparing for an audition.

For the young performer reading this book, I have three tips to share with you to help you get the most out of these monologues…

THREE TIPS FOR YOUNG PERFORMERS

1. **Understand the character.**

Start with the words. The words are the foundation upon which you build your character. If you don't know what a word means, look it up. If you don't know how to pronounce a word, ask someone for help or go on YouTube and find a pronunciation video. Do this before your audition or first rehearsal; the director will appreciate that you've done your homework.

The character. Now analyse the character from all angles. Analyse their words, actions, thoughts and feelings at different points. Understand them. *Empathise* with them. Why do they feel and act as they do? What is their backstory? What motivates them? Do they have an objective? What do they love? What do they fear? Being able to answer these questions will help you to develop a nuanced, engaging performance.

Stage directions. If there is a 'beat', it signals a pause in which the character is thinking, reacting or experiencing some kind of emotional shift – these moments are important. Don't make the mistake of rushing through the piece without pause for thought, as it gives the impression that you are reciting memorised lines. To make a character real, the audience must see a thought process.

Further research. You may need to study an accent, research a historical time, read a play, or analyse a real person's behaviour. To play Abraham Lincoln, you would need to understand the historical context of the US Civil War. To play the Queen of England, you would need to study her mannerisms and speech. To play a Shakespearean character, you would need to read the full play. This will enhance the authenticity of your performance.

2. Feel the words.

Many performers can memorise lines and relevant actions, but it takes special skill to convey emotion. When a laugh or cry comes across as fake, it is because the actor is *pretending* to laugh or *pretending* to cry. But the best actors in the world are the best because they're not pretending. They use their real emotions and instincts, drawn from their own experiences, to portray what their character is feeling.

This is why Meryl Streep says, 'Acting is not about being someone different. It's finding the similarity in what is apparently different, then finding myself in there.' It is also the basis of Sanford Meisner's theory that 'Acting is behaving truthfully under imaginary circumstances.' So, get in touch with your emotions (and the memories and thoughts that prompt them), and think about where you can find yourself in the monologue.

3. Be creative.

How will you use the stage? How will you use movement, expression, gesture, volume, tone, pace, pauses, props? How will you engage the audience? Don't give a performance all on one level; find the nuances and take the audience on a rollercoaster ride. Create suspense (a dramatic pause!). Create tension (increase pace or volume or urgency). Create rapport (eye contact, audience interaction). When you are developing your performance, experiment. Try different things. Be thoughtful and creative, and make sure your creative decisions have a rationale.

For more tips and resources, I run a blog offering audition and acting advice, strategies for learning lines, monologue videos and more at www.buddingtheatre.com

Good luck with your performance – have fun!

Kirsty Budding 2019

FANTASY & fairy tales

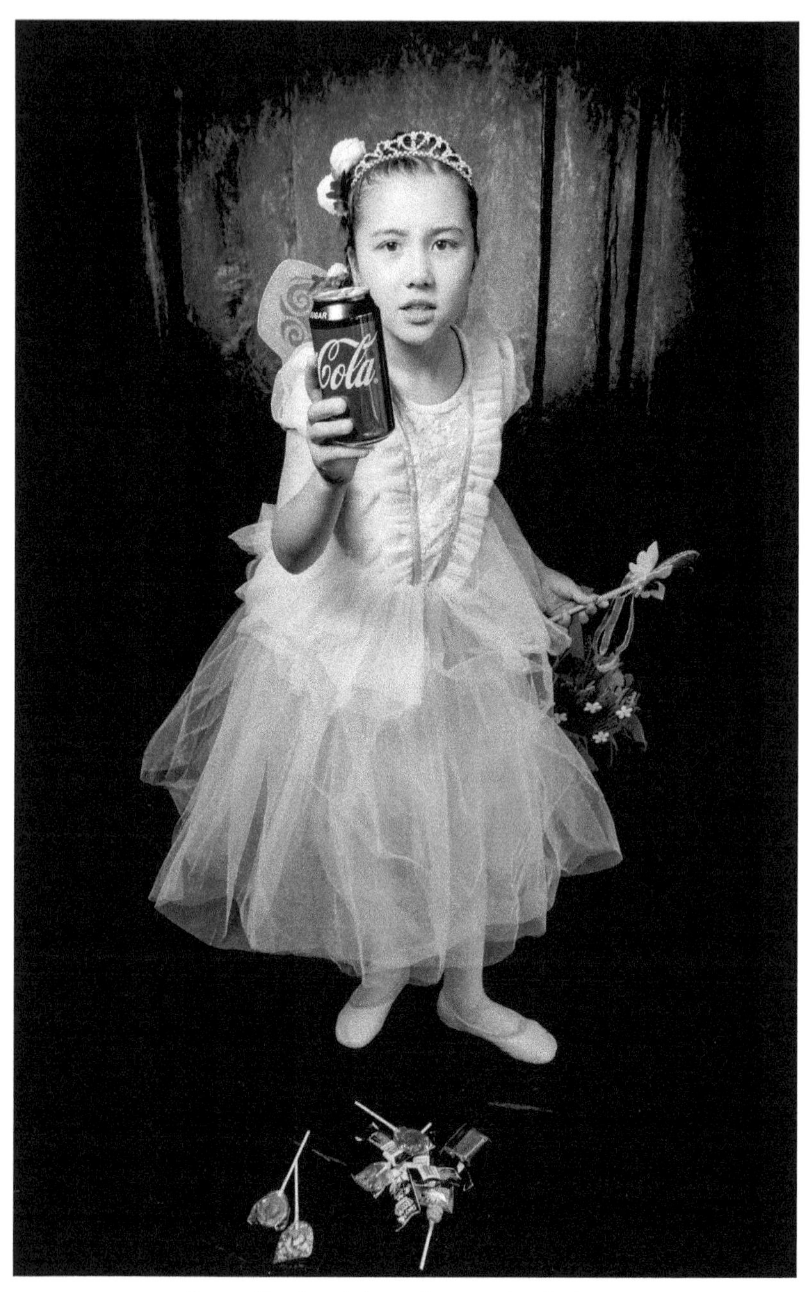

Crystelle Cox (8) performs 'Tooth Fairy'

BAD FAIRY

(Comedy/Drama)

A LITTLE FAIRY stands, arms folded, very displeased.

The fairy teacher put me in time out. (*with attitude*) I didn't even do anything... except throw some fairy dust at the teacher which... (*giggling mischievously*) turned her into an elephant. (*earnestly*) But apart from that, I'm innocent! (*thoughtfully*) I just find it a bit difficult to concentrate. I'm not very good at fairy maths, (*sadly*) or anything really. So, I guess I'll just stay in time out forever. (*sits, buries head in hands)*

LITTLE WIZARD

(Drama)

A LITTLE WIZARD enters

I'm a little wizard and I can make magic! I can fly on a broomstick above the clouds! I can do magic spells that turn vegetables into chocolate! I can wave my wand and get anything I want! (*smile falls; and then, sadly)* But, unfortunately, my magic can't make people love each other, so I guess I'll be alone forever. (*exits sadly)*

HAPPY MERMAID

(Comedy)

A HAPPY MERMAID enters.

My favourite animals are seahorses, which is lucky because I live in the sea! I'm a mermaid and, though I like the sea, sometimes I dream of going up on the land… (*looks up dreamily, then frowns*) Then I remember what happened to Ariel, and I'm like: no thank you! I don't want to marry a prince and have ugly human feet! Ew! I'm staying RIGHT HERE!

ANGRY MERMAID

(Drama)

A MERMAID glares at the audience, outraged.

What are YOU doing here? This is MY secret lagoon! Read that sign right there! (*points to a sign*) NO HUMANS ALLOWED. Because we all know what happens when humans get involved. You throw away your straws which get stuck up the poor turtles' noses! You cast your nets which trap the dolphins! You leave your rubbish which makes the seagulls sick. That's why I hide in my secret lagoon, (*sadly*) but soon... there won't be anywhere left to hide. So stay and have a picnic, and leave your rubbish behind. I know a sign won't stop you.

OGRE
(Comedy)

An OGRE stands reading a book.

'An ogre is a legendary monster usually depicted as a large, hideous, beast that eats humans, especially children.' (*looks up*) That is SO untrue! OK, maybe I live in a swamp and maybe I'm a little bit smelly and a little bit grumpy, but I would never eat a human! They would taste disgusting! I'm tired of all this blatant, anti-ogre prejudice. (*with great dignity*) Now, if you'll excuse me, I'm going to take a mud bath.

TOOTH FAIRY
(Comedy)

The TOOTH FAIRY has the manner of a strict school teacher.

Hello. I am the Tooth Fairy. Though I may look young, I've been doing this job for a very long time and it's fair to say, I am appalled. Chocolates. Lolly pops. Coca Cola. I think you know what I'm talking about. That's right: gum disease. Have you ever put a tooth in a can of coke and left it for a few days to see what happens? It's pretty gross. So, cut the sugary snacks and make sure you spend at least two minutes brushing, twice per day – especially the back molars as that's where cavities develop. Take my advice, or you won't get a cent from me! Good day!

FAIRY GODMOTHER

(Comedy)

FAIRY GODMOTHER looks at her wand, frustrated.

Work you stupid wand! *(notices audience)* Oh, hello! I'm Fairy Godmother! I'm just having a bit of trouble with my magic wand. You see, I wanted to help Cinderella go to the ball! But when I tried to turn a pumpkin into a carriage, I just turned the pumpkin into a big, talking pumpkin! Now he won't shut up! And the glass slippers are a pair of Nikes. It's a disaster. Oh well. *(shouts)* Cinderella! You'll have to sprint to the ball! You're wearing Nikes! Just do it!

FAIRY SPOKESPERSON

(Comedy)

A FAIRY in a business suit enters carrying a clipboard.

Quiet please. (*Importantly*) I am a spokesperson for the Magical Fairy Kingdom and I am here to negotiate terms. We, the fairies, are unhappy with the current arrangements and have the following list of demands. (*puts on glasses, reads*) Number One. The Tooth Fairy has noticed a decline in the quality of teeth under pillows. Therefore, children should not have sugary drinks, or you won't get a cent from us. (*refers to list*) Number Two. Fairy Godmother would like it known that she can turn a pumpkin into a carriage, but she cannot turn a pumpkin into an Audi R8. Please stop requesting this. (*refers to list*) Number Three. Tinkerbell would like everyone to know that she is not in love with Peter Pan, because he is: quote (*reads quote*) "super immature." Please adjust your productions of Peter Pan accordingly. (*takes off glasses*) That will be all for now. Please meet our demands, (*darkly*) or else. (*smiles*) Thank you.

PALACE ANNOUNCER

(Comedy)

The PALACE ANNOUNCER is like a gameshow host.

Ladies and gentleman, boys and girls, I'm pleased to present his royal majesty, the host of the ball, the man we're all here to see, Priiiiiiiiince Charming! (*holds out arm to the door as if expecting Prince Charming to enter, but he doesn't, so delivers the line again in the same energetic, expectant way*) ... Priiiiiiiiince Charming! (*looks around*). Um, it looks like Prince Charming is running late. He's probably straightening his hair. This is awkward. So, I'll just fill in... um.... (*trying to think of something to say*) he's a great guy, that Prince Charming. You know, he was recently featured on Channel Ten's 'The Bachelor Prince' and Channel Nine's 'The Charmer Wants a Wife'! Did anyone watch? No, the ratings were terrible. (*Looks at watch*) Oh, this is ridiculous! I quit.

JEALOUS QUEEN

(Comedy)

The QUEEN is flicking through a women's magazine.

I see Rapunzel's launched a new range of shampoos: (*mimics advertisement*) 'Your hair will grow long enough for a man to climb up it!'. Ew. And Snow White is still pushing her skin brightening cream. What a sell-out. (*turns page*) Ooo, gossip! Apparently, Cinderella and Prince Charming have been spending time apart. There she is on a beach in St Tropez! She looks like she's put on weight. Good. (*turns page*) Who wore it better? Belle in the original movie or Belle in the remake. Original Belle, obviously! But I hate them both. (*turns page*) No Ariel, I don't want to buy one of your shell bikinis. Clearly photoshopped. (*turns page*) Ooo horoscopes! I don't believe in them but I read them anyway. (*reads*) This week, beware the green-eyed monster as fortune favours the good. (*looks up sceptically*) What a load of rubbish.

GENIE

(Comedy/Drama)

The GENIE begins crouched on the floor – their back to the audience – then with a yawn they grow into a full height genie. The GENIE turns around to face the audience.

Who summons the powerful, magical, amazing blue genie of the lamp? (*Looks at someone in the audience, unimpressed*) Oh, you? Really? I was hoping for someone more impressive. I hope you're going to wish for some new clothes. That can be your first wish. Did I mention you have three wishes? That's right. I have the power to grant three wishes. But ONLY three. Please read the small print: no wishing for more wishes and no exchanges or refunds. So what would you like to wish for? A designer bag? A red Ferrari? A palace? (*reading their expression*) Or something more...? Something money can't buy? Yes, I see what you wish for, Aladdin. You wish for love.

ZOMBIE

(Comedy)

A ZOMBIE tells an epic tale.

The world ended last night. The age of the zombies has begun. They crawl over buildings, finding their way in to claim whoever is left. Last night, I joined them, but the problem is... (*breaks character; becomes casual and animated*) I just don't fit it! The other zombies are bigger and scarier than me. They move faster. They make these zombie sounds like (*imitates zombie*) 'Muuaaurrgghhhhhh' but when it comes time to show off my zombie skills, all I can manage is (*make pathetic zombie sound*) 'Mwerrrr'. The other zombies laugh at me. I didn't even know zombies could laugh! The most embarrassing thing is that I don't want to chase humans... I just want to eat carrots. I'm a vegetarian zombie, but I can't let them find out! Wish me luck. (*walks off like a scary zombie*).

HARRY POTTER'S SUCCESSOR

(Comedy)

A YOUNG PERSON dressed in black robes paces up and down with anxiousness and excitement.

Shouldn't be long now. It's way past my eleventh birthday. I live in the suburbs. It's summer. It shouldn't be long. (*looks at watch*) Don't know why I'm looking at my watch. I don't know what time it will happen. (*looks up quickly)* Is that an owl? ... No, no it's a seagull. (*brings attention back*) My parents think I'm mad (*mimicking parents*) 'You're obsessed with that book! It's not real! Get your head out of the clouds and into the real world!' They keep trying to stop me from sleeping under the stairs... but they'll see. I've been trying to discover my magical powers. When we eat dinner, I try to summon the tomato ketchup with the power of my mind. Usually Dad just passes it to me though. Yesterday, I tried to transfigure my cat but, she just hissed at me. And when we went to the zoo, I spent an hour in the reptile house trying to speak Parseltongue. Management asked me to leave. Still, I won't give up! I'm going to stand here waiting for my letter from Hogwarts all summer. Because I know I have magical powers. I just know it. (*pulls out a wand and points it*) Wingardium Leviosa! (*beat*) Yeah, nothing.

GREEK &
NORSE
MYTHOLOGY

Toby Gosling-Dunlop (10) as Loki and Harper Scott (9) as Thor

THOR

(Comedy)

THOR enters wearing a red cape, possibly carrying an underwhelming toy hammer.

I know what you're thinking: 'You don't look like Thor. Where are your muscles? Why don't you have a deep voice?' If I ever meet Chris Hemsworth, I'm going to give him a piece of my mind. He's completely ruined my life! Let's get the facts straight. Thor means thunder. You don't need to be able to bench press a car when you can strike people with lightning. I create quite a lot of storms; if you ever have a power cut, sorry, that was me. It mainly happens when I'm in a bad mood because someone compared me to Chris Hemsworth. Or when I get in trouble for fighting with my brother. His name's Loki and he's super annoying. He's always pulling my hair and stealing my toys and planning world domination. Just to annoy him, I always tell him he's adopted. Anyway, I better go; I want to go and spy on Loki. He's playing over the road with the frost giants; and I don't trust them. Bye!

LOKI
(Comedy)

LOKI enters wearing a green cape.

My brother is an idiot. He's always spying on me when I go and play with my friends, the frost giants. They're nice kids, they're just misunderstood! AND he keeps stealing my tesseract and hiding it where I can't reach. That's mine and I got it for my birthday! I've told mum but she never listens to me. She just says, (*mimics*) 'Play nicely with your brother!' Yeah, I would if he didn't keep striking me with lightning! Such favouritism. Of course, they deny that Thor's the favourite: (*mimics*) 'We love you both the same', but parents always say that. They definitely have a favourite. So, I've been considering my options, and me and the frost giants have planned a funny prank. But don't tell Thor, OK? Let's see how smug he is without his precious hammer. (*evil laughs*) Gotta go.

POSEIDON

(Comedy)

POSEIDON, God of the Sea, stares grimly.

I have seaweed in my hair. It smells like… seaweed. The other gods think being God of the Sea must be cool but, actually, it stinks. Literally, I smell like fish. And you won't believe what I have to put up with: cheeky dolphins always making jokes at my expense; jellyfish stinging my butt; noisy boats waking me up, and plastic bags littering my garden! I've had enough! So, I've decided to go for a holiday in the Caribbean! (*puts on sunglasses*) Say hello to Poseidon, God of the Beach!

DIONYSUS

(Comedy)

DIONYSUS is singing and dancing.

Celebrate good times, come on! Ba ba ba ba ba ba ba ba! (*notices audience*) Oh hi, I'm Dionysus, God of Celebrations and Wine! Except this is a kid's monologue, so I'm the God of Celebrations and Red Cordial! If you ever need a party planner, look me up. I'm available for birthdays, holidays, christenings, and even funerals if you really didn't like them. Don't be a party pooper, call 0800 DIONYSUS now!

HADES

(Comedy)

HADES, God of the Underworld, enters.

Let me tell you how I became God of the Underworld. I was the eldest son of the gods Cronus and Rhea. They were the Titans! Then there was this HUGE fight between The Titans and their kids, and basically we won. Also Dad tried to eat us which was awkward — And LONG STORY SHORT, me and my brothers Zeus and Poseidon defeated our parents and took over the world! Then we had to decide who would rule over the sea, who would rule over the sky and who would rule over the Underworld... (*quiet for a moment, haunted by the memory*) I will never regret anything more than that game of 'rock, paper, scissors'. So, Poseidon won the sea, Zeus won the sky, and I got stuck with... (*looks around grimly*) an underground cave full of dead people.

APHRODITE

(Comedy)

APHRODITE is like a high school gossip girl.

So I'm actually a really important goddess, probably more important than any other god, actually. I'm definitely the most popular goddess, because I'm Aphrodite! Goddess of Love! In fact, it was ME who found Zeus his wife, Hera! Actually, between us, things haven't been going well with them lately. They're seeing the God of Marriage Counselling. Something about Zeus having a secret child called Hercules. Awkward. Anyway, I better go. Love is in the air!

ZEUS

(Comedy)

ZEUS, God of the Sky, holds up a cardboard lightning bolt.

(*Impressively, in a booming voice*) I am Zeus, God of the Sky! Look how strong I am! Look how effortlessly I hold up this huge lightning bolt! (*gives up, dropping the act*). OK, OK, it's made of cardboard. I'm just trying to impress the other gods. My brother Hades is always picking on me for being God of the Sky. He calls me 'the weather reporter'. (*turns into a weather reporter, using thunderbolt to point to imaginary map*) We can expect medium to light showers across the region today accompanied by easterly winds and, given what I had for breakfast, there is likely to be occasional thunder. (*thunder bolt becomes microphone*) Zeus reporting, now back to the studio!

HERCULES

(Comedy)

HERCULES is upbeat and ready to show off his muscles.

Hi, I'm Hercules! I don't know if you're aware of this, but I'm kind of a big deal. Half god, half mortal, (*shows off*) huge muscles, excellent athletic ability. Yeah, I've got it pretty good. I did have one challenge though: the Nemean Lion. Everyone was like: 'Kill the lion, Hercules!' and I was like, 'No way! Look how cute he is! He looks like Puss in Boots!' So, I pretended to kill the lion, but I secretly adopted him. His name's Bob. Bob the Lion. The moral of this story is: adopt, don't shop! You too can have a Bob, by visiting your local animal rescue service. (*exits waving*) Stay in school, kids!

HERA

(Comedy)

HERA stares grimly.

Hi. I'm Hera. I'm Queen of the Gods, although everyone seems to forget that and just calls me (*scathingly*) 'Zeus' Mrs'. I basically sit on Mount Olympus eating chocolate while reflecting on my poor life choices. Zeus has soooo many ex-girlfriends, and I'm not cool with that! Like, the other day, he said 'Remember that awesome time we went and watched the Olympics?' and I was like, 'No, Zeus, you're thinking of a date with your ex-girlfriend again. That was a thousand years ago. I hate sport!' (*takes a big breath*) Luckily, I have two things to comfort me: chocolate, and vengeance. (*eats chocolate while contemplating vengeance*).

CUPID

(Comedy/Drama)

CUPID flies in.

Hi! I'm Cupid, and my job is to make people fall in love! How it works is: I shoot you with my bow and arrow! It doesn't hurt when it hits you, but it feels like your heart is beating really fast. It feels like you see everything you ever wanted in front of you. It feels like you have a chance to live your dream life, with someone who will give you lots of cuddles and make you tea when you're sad. It feels like you can never let them go. So, if you ever feel this way, you'll know you just got shot by a cute kid with wings! (*flutters away*)

NARCISSUS

(Comedy)

NARCISSUS holds phone aloft, posing.

I wish I could talk but, I'm kind of busy. My name's Narcissus; you may have heard the story of how I fell in love with my reflection. Well, technology has improved since then! I've been taking this selfie for over a thousand years, trying to get it just right. The right lighting, the right look, the right hashtags. But now I've been staring at myself so long that no filter can make me look young again. It's OK, I'm sure the Russian government will release a more effective filter app soon. (*exits pulling duck faces at phone*)

MEDUSA

(Drama)

MEDUSA – hair full of snakes – reads from a phone.

(*reading*) 'In Greek mythology, Medusa was a monster, a Gorgon, generally described as a woman with living snakes in place of hair. A man hater, all those who gazed upon her face would turn to stone.' (*stops reading; looks up*) That's me, according to Wikipedia. Well, here's a few things you might not know about me. I was the mother of Pegasus – that's right, the cute flying horse from 'Hercules'. I was also chased by Poseidon, God of the Sea, who had a bit of a thing for me, and Athena got super jealous. I didn't even like Poseidon! He smelt like fish! And he had seaweed in his beard. But Athena was like: 'It's YOUR FAULT, Medusa! It's your fault that he likes you! It's because your hair is so beautiful! (*coldly*) We'll have to do something about that.' So Athena turned my hair into snakes, and I was banished to an island. I was angry. Men invaded my island every week because they made a bet they could kill me, because nothing says 'masculinity' like killing a woman – right? So, I turned them all to stone. And everyone said: 'Medusa, why are you so angry?' I became a symbol of angry women everywhere. The Evil Medusa who turns men to stone. Fortunately, things have changed. People started to discover my side of the story. I became a symbol of justice. I'm also a logo on Versace handbags, so I guess being a female boss with hair made out of snakes is back in fashion. Come visit me if you want, but be careful… I'm angry, and I bite.

SECRET AGENTS
and
ESPIONAGE

Sam Welling (13) as the 'Assassin'

LOLLIES TAKEN

(Comedy)

SOMEONE's lollies have been taken.

My lollies… have been taken. (*lifts phone to ear*) I don't know who you are. If you are looking for ransom, I can tell you I don't have money. But what I do have are a very particular set of skills, skills I have acquired over a very long career of eating lollies. Skills that make me a nightmare for lolly thieves like you. If you give me back my lollies, that'll be the end of it. I will not look for you, I will not pursue you. But if you don't, I will look for you, I will find you, and I will tell the teacher on you.

ASSASSIN

(Comedy)

An ASSASSIN in a suit enters.

You've heard of John Wick, right? Well, I trained him. (*nods seriously*) That's right. I'm an assassin, and just like John Wick, I drive a very cool car and own a very cute puppy. Some people don't approve of my profession, but you're lucky I'm around because there are some bad people out there. People who eat popcorn a bit too loudly at the movies. People who play on their phones even though the trailers clearly told them not to. People who open a noisy packet of chips during a quiet, intense scene. People who slurp a giant coke and then leave the coke in the cup holder, hoping no one will notice, because it's dark. So next time you go to the movies, remember I'll be there, hiding in the shadows, watching. (*does 'I'm watching you' hand signal)*

JAMES BLONDE

(Comedy)

A SECRET AGENT enters carrying a juice box.

Hi, I'm Blonde – (*drinks noisily through straw*) – James Blonde. Come here. (*invites the audience to come in closer*) You won't tell, will you? Cause this is top secret. (*looks left and right*) I'm a secret agent. That's right. I travel around the world in my fast car – (*say quickly*) and by the world, I mean, my school, and by fast car I mean, my legs – winning the hearts of year nine girls with my cute smile and overactive imagination! Today's mission? Ask Jane Brown to go on a date with me... (*walks purposefully as if going to ask her, but then stops – hopeless*) But the mission will fail because she's going to say no. She likes that annoying boy, Josh, who always gets kicked out of class. What is it about girls liking bad boys? When I'm an international man of mystery, Josh will be living in a trailer playing Xbox because he never learnt how to read. Josh thinks Jane is hot. Everyone thinks Jane is hot. But I don't think she's hot... I think she's beautiful. (*beat*) It's OK. I'll ask her tomorrow. I've been saying that since Year 7. I'll ask her tomorrow. (*with dignity*) Now, if you'll excuse me, I'm getting in my Aston Martin. (*acts out getting in Aston Martin and driving off*)

RUSSIAN AUSSIE SPY

(Comedy)

A RUSSIAN SPY enters.

(*In a Russian accent*) I was given this mission six months ago: (*reads secret note*) 'Go to Australia. Infiltrate notorious gang to steal secrets for Mother Russia.' Now I am here, posing as new Australian gang member. No one suspects me. Why would they? I am chameleon. Let me demonstrate. (*completely changes posture and expression, speaking with a strong, Australian accent*) G'day mate! How ya goin'? Put another shrimp on the barby! That's not a knife; this is a knife! She'll be right! Fair dinkum. All good, mate! Let's get Maccas in the arvo and then go to the servo to see Wayno. Servo's just past the bottle-o. Chuck a U-E at the lights. No worries, mate! (*switches back suddenly to his Russian persona*) You see? I am natural. Unfortunately, there is snag in my plan... I have fallen in love with enemy's beautiful daughter. When I first saw her, I said: (*in Australian accent*) You're a good lookin', Sheila! (*in Russian accent*) And she said: (*mimicking a woman with a strong Australian accent*) Do you even lift, bro? (*In a Russian accent*) And I said: (*Australian accent*) Nah, mate. (*Russian accent*) So now, my mission has changed. I must get big muscles so that beautiful Australian girl will marry me. Wish me luck, mate.

comedy

Alex Peek (13) and Robert Wearden (17),
both performers of 'School Principal'

MATH CLASS

(Comedy)

A STUDENT in math class.

I don't plan on being an engineer, architect, builder, or landscape gardener, so why do I need to be able to calculate the angle of a triangle? I'm pretty sure I'm never going to go for a job interview and be asked to 'find the angle of x'. And these ridiculous problems! (*reads*) 'John has two containers of punch. One is 5% juice, the other is 10% juice. How much of each should John mix together to get a 10-litre solution of 7% juice?' I don't know, John, maybe just go get a Boost juice or something? What do you need ten litres of 7% juice for anyway? Are you some kind of juice deviant? And DON'T get me started on calculus.

DIVA

(Comedy)

An outraged DIVA.

What do you mean I didn't get the part?! Who else could you possibly cast in the lead role? (*listens*) ASHLEY?! As if! Her dancing was like this: (*dances very badly*) Whereas my dancing was like this: (*dances amazingly*). And her singing, was like this: (*sings badly*) But my singing, was like this: (*belts out a vocally challenging song e.g. "I Will Always Love You" or a popular musical number*). And her acting was like: (*acts out opening line badly, like a robot with no expression*) 'What. Do. You. Mean. I. Didn't. Get. The. Part.' Whereas my acting was like this: (*a dramatic outburst identical to the opening line*) 'What do you mean I didn't get the part?!'

AUSTRALIA'S GOT TALENT

(Comedy)

A KID enters, lost and confused.

Hello? I'm looking for a toilet— (*sees audience; asks individuals*) Have you seen a toilet? What about you? Why is there an audience? (*looks to the centre*) And judges? (*looks to the side*) And a camera? (*smiles awkwardly*) This isn't the toilet, is it. I must have stopped at the wrong floor. (*starts to exit, then stops suddenly and looks back at the judges*) No! This isn't my act. What do you mean four out of ten?! I'll show you! (*Does a crazy dance, but still needs the toilet so dances oddly*) Yeah! Check out this talent! (*finishes dance with a pose*) SO what's my score? ... ONE out of ten?! Are you serious?! You don't know talent when you see it! Amateurs! (*exits awkwardly*)

PRIMARY SCHOOL TEACHER

(Comedy)

A PRIMARY SCHOOL TEACHER with a coffee cup.

Primary school children are so loud. They're just SO loud! And energetic! Where does the energy come from? It's like they suck it out of me! Yeah, I know what you're thinking: you chose this career! This is me when I was younger (*imitates very sweet idealistic person with a high pitched voice*) I can't wait to be a primary school teacher and inspire little children! It will be SO rewarding! (*drops the act*) Ha! This morning, one kid asked to go to the toilet, then ALL the kids decided they wanted to go to the toilet. There was literally a stampede. I was almost mowed down by five year olds. Then, when I finished managing the (*shudders*) mess, I saw a boy eating his maths book. Just munching on it like a camel at a zoo. That was hard to explain to his mum. So you may be wondering, how do I survive? (*looks at cup*) That's right. Coffee. (*looks at watch*) Wish me luck. Recess is over. (*takes a swig and exits fearfully)*

LOST IN THE LOUVRE

(Comedy)

A SCHOOL STUDENT enters, panicked, speaking fast.

Hi! I don't want to freak you out but I'm on a school excursion and I'm lost! I don't know what happened; I was just standing in the gallery with the Mona Lisa, you know the room where like a million people take photos of this tiny painting for some reason; and then I turned around and my teacher was gone and my friends were gone, and we were planning to go to the Eiffel Tower next and I do NOT want to miss that so, I know I'm a bit old for this, but could you please do some kind of announcement over the PA? (*beat*) Oh, sorry, you don't speak English. Um… Bonjour! Mon… friends… no, mes amis! Mes amis, they went 'Au revoir' and now I am très freaked out because I want to get le photograph in front of le Eiffel Tower for le Instagram. Comprenez vous? (*sees school friends offstage*) Oh, there they are! (*running off*) Merci beaucoup!

UNWILLING ACTOR
(Comedy)

A BOY - wearing a red wig.

I don't want to be an actor. No, seriously. It's all my Mum. It started when I was five: (*mimics mother's voice*) 'You're going to have drama lessons to improve your confidence!' Before long, she had me auditioning for every show in town, even for roles I clearly wasn't suited for, like Annie. I don't have red hair, I can't sing, I can't tap dance, and I'm a boy. Recently, it's gotten worse. She's been calling agents. I've got auditions for drama schools next week. And all I want to do is say, 'Mum, I don't want to be an actor! It's not my dream, it's yours.' She won't listen because she thinks my dream is stupid. It's so out there, I'm afraid to say it out loud... but, I dream of the bright lights of accountancy! Filling in tax forms. Using math in my everyday work. What could be more rewarding? But my mum would never allow it. So, I have no choice but to become a movie star, get an Oscar, and dream of what could have been.

NOT DISNEYLAND

(Comedy)

A KID stands dressed in Disney merchandise.

This is an outrage. Seriously. Where is Belle? Sleeping Beauty? Pocahontas? Cinderella? I don't get it. My parents are acting so weird. Guys, I don't want to see Scooby Doo, OK. I'm not into cartoon dogs. They're trying to distract me: (*imitates*) 'why don't you have a photo with Optimus Prime?' Who on earth is Optimus Prime?! (*Sees giant robot*) Oh, a giant robot. No thanks. I want fairytales! I would also settle for meeting the cast of High School Musical. (*Sings*) 'We're all in this together...' (*bored*) No, I don't want to see King Kong in 3-D. No, I don't want to go on a Jurassic Park ride. The Fast and the Furious?! As if! This Disney Land is terrible. We should get our money back. (*beat*) Suddenly, Mum and Dad look a bit awkward, like they're scared to tell me something. Like they're regretting making that impulsive promise on my birthday last year. Like they hoped I wouldn't notice. Avoiding eye contact, they point at a sign up high over the Transformers display. And there it is. In big black letters. The words that will ruin my day and possibly my whole life: Welcome to Universal Studios.

MOODY QUEEN

(Comedy)

The QUEEN enters, giving the audience the Queen's wave, her movement poised and face serene. Then – she gives up; moodily, she cradles her hand like it hurts and starts walking like a slovenly commoner. Only her plummy accent remains.

Another day waving. Another day smiling. Another day cutting ribbons and planting trees and receiving flowers from ugly children. (*looks at watch*) Urgh. Now I have to meet the new Prime Minister. ANOTHER one! Honestly, I was hoping I would be dead by now. I think my son was too. (*thoughtfully, sincerely*) Poor Charles, what a loser he is. Always waiting there in the wings. (*If actually being performed; from the wings, CHARLES calls: 'Hello Mummy!'*) Hello Charles. (*distracted by her sleeve*) Look at this! Mud! I don't know why they keep making me plant trees. I'm ninety-three years old and I've got fifty gardeners just walking aimlessly around the grounds of Buckingham Palace. (*looks offstage*) Did you hear that? The butler is showing in the Prime Minister. It will take them another minute to reach the door. I had better do my homework. (*picks up a newspaper; puts on glasses and reads*) Boris. What a stupid name. I give him a month.

MESSY ROOM

(Comedy)

A YOUNG PERSON stands, outraged. The following monologue is directed at their mother – the audience.

I'm not allowed out until I tidy my room?! But Mum! It's not even that bad! OK, maybe I left a few clothes on the floor… actually, I don't remember what the floor looks like. Was the carpet grey or beige? But apart from that, it's fiiiine. (*listens; then matter-of-factly*) Yes, there are sixteen empty mugs on the bedside table, but so what? I like tea! What do you expect me to do? Wash one up every time I want to use one?! And yes, there are wrappers on the floor – I mean, on the clothes – and empty shopping bags and a thousand pairs of shoes and the school uniform I didn't put in the wash. And yes, my bed is so covered in clothes, damp towels and technological devices that it resembles the nest of a disorganised magpie. And maybe there is some leftover pizza from when I had a movie marathon, and maybe a few crumbs are currently being carried down the hall by a trail of ants heading back to their colony… but apart from that, (*with dignity*) my bedroom… is like a palace!

HELPING GRANDMA

(Comedy)

A YOUNG PERSON is on the phone.

OK Grandma, press the 'ON' button. Done it? Good, now, log in. Move the mouse... (*exasperated*) the white thing on the square foam thing – move that and click on 'log in.' Now, you'll probably see the Antivirus program start up. You don't need to do anything with that, OK, so just close the window. (*waits; no reply*) Grandma? Did you hear me? Grandma? (*she's back*) Where did you go? (*beat*) Grandma, I meant close the window on the computer. How would it help to close the living room window? How would I even know it was open? It doesn't matter. Click the X in the top right hand corner. Done that? OK. Now go to the start menu – it's in the bottom left-hand corner. You'll see a space that says, 'Type here to search.' I need you to click in that box and type in 'Skype.' S-K-Y-P-E. (*Waits, then quietly exasperated*) The 'S' is on the middle row of the keyboard, on the left. Next to the 'A'. The 'K' is on the same row on the right. The last three letters are all on the top row. (*Waits, looks at watch*) Do you see it? Skype? Click on it! Alright! I'm going to call you. Hold on a minute. (*Hangs up, then looks at their phone*). Hi Grandma! Can you see me? I can see you! Or I can see your forehead, at least. And the ceiling. It's like magic, isn't it! See, now isn't this easier than using the phone?

SCHOOL PRINCIPAL

(Comedy)

The SCHOOL PRINCIPAL addresses their students – the audience.

Alright settle down, settle down. I know you're all keen to go home, but it's important that in assembly we are attentive and respectful until the very end.

As your new Principal, I have been delighted with your behaviour in the first week back. I have only had the police called to the school grounds twice this week and just one teacher has had a mental breakdown. Give yourselves a pat on the back.

I'll keep this brief; I have some housekeeping notes on etiquette in the playground, and— (*stops abruptly*) I notice as I speak that most of you are playing on your phones. I believe strongly in treating you like adults, which is why we don't have consequences for bad behaviour at this school, however I must insist that you put your phones away, right now. (*beat*)

I see that you're so engrossed in your phones that you did not hear me, and I am in fact giving this speech to myself and the three or so students at the front who will make it to university. If you persist in not listening, I will be forced to raise my voice.

(*Waits, then raises voice*) There will be consequences for phone use while the Principal is speaking! Don't push me, students. I am not afraid to make empty threats to contact your parents. (*points to someone in the audience*) That includes you, Brayden. I see you swiping up and down; loading and reloading. You don't have any Facebook notifications; no one cares.

Now we need to discuss the playground, and by the playground I of course mean the car park. You are kindly requested not to loiter in your cars or play offensive music loudly near the classrooms. I have been told that several math classes have been disrupted by the pervasive beats of… (*reads off paper and mispronounces 'Kanye'*) Kanye West. Ah, you find that funny. Well, you know kids, I was young once too. I too listened to music while driving in cars. My friends and I would go out in my Mum's old Ford listening to 'sick beats' like Donny Osmond's 'Puppy Love'. Those were wild times, I can tell you! Now none of you are listening. Apparently, you don't care that I used to be young, in fact it makes you respect me less.

Fine. Well, nothing makes people listen like the truth, so here goes: I'm the Principal and I lack principals. I didn't become a teacher because I had a calling or even because I liked children; I became a teacher because I gave up on my dreams. I have low expectations of your achievement because you're at the tail-end of the socio-economic bell curve, and I'm just doing my time here before I can get a job at a private school. And I won't miss you, because I'll see you every day when I get my drive-through coffee at Maccas.

And look at that – you're all listening! Well done. All that remains for me to say is: GET TO CLASS!

NATIVITY DIRECTOR

(Comedy)

The NATIVITY DIRECTOR addresses their cast – the audience.

So, this is it. Opening Night. We've rehearsed for three months and, uh, well – we can't do much about it now. How do you all feel? ...Good? Really? After that dress rehearsal?

I just wanted to chat to you before the show because a lot of work has gone into this. A lot of blood, sweat and tears. And I wanted to tell you that, (*as if about to reassure them*) whatever happens on stage tonight, even if the production is a complete disaster… it will not be my fault.

With this in mind, here are my notes from the dress rehearsal. (*refers to clipboard*) Joseph, you missed your cue. Again. How hard is it to remember that when the Angel Gabriel – (*picks on someone in the audience*) looking at you, Billy – I've never seen such a bland interpretation of an angel – when the Angel Gabriel exits, that's your cue to kneel down and look up at the sky. And when you kneel, can you please remember to kneel *in profile* rather than with your back to the audience? And that goes for all of you. If you're speaking to the back of the stage or the floor (*picks on someone in the audience*) or your hand, for some reason, Wise Man Number One, then the audience can't hear you.

(*Refers to list*) Props. I don't recall the baby Jesus receiving the gifts of gold, frankincense and a hand full of nothing! (*Picks on someone in the audience*) Where is your myrrh, Wise Man Number Three? I don't want to hear excuses; just get your act together.

(*Refers to list*) The closing song. I don't know where to begin. You seem to have all forgotten how to move, how to smile, and how to sing. ENERGY! If you don't seriously lift your game, I will make an announcement over the PA telling the audience to google a video of paint drying to keep them entertained for those four appalling minutes.

The only thing that surpasses the closing song in lack of coordination is the final bow. What the HELL was that. I've told you a hundred times, you have to wait for the leader in the centre to bow, which is (*picks on someone in the audience*) Sebastian. Sebastian, you were only given this role because you're tall, not because you have any talent. Do not bow until everyone is on stage.

(*Sincerely*) Finally, I'd just like to give a warm thank you… to the cleaners. Rob and Wendy. You've done a wonderful job cleaning up after rehearsals. If only the performers were as thorough with their lines as you are with your vacuum cleaners. (*claps*) Clap everyone! Show your appreciation for the cleaners!

(*Drops smile*) Now, get backstage. Your parents will be arriving soon.

Christmas
themed

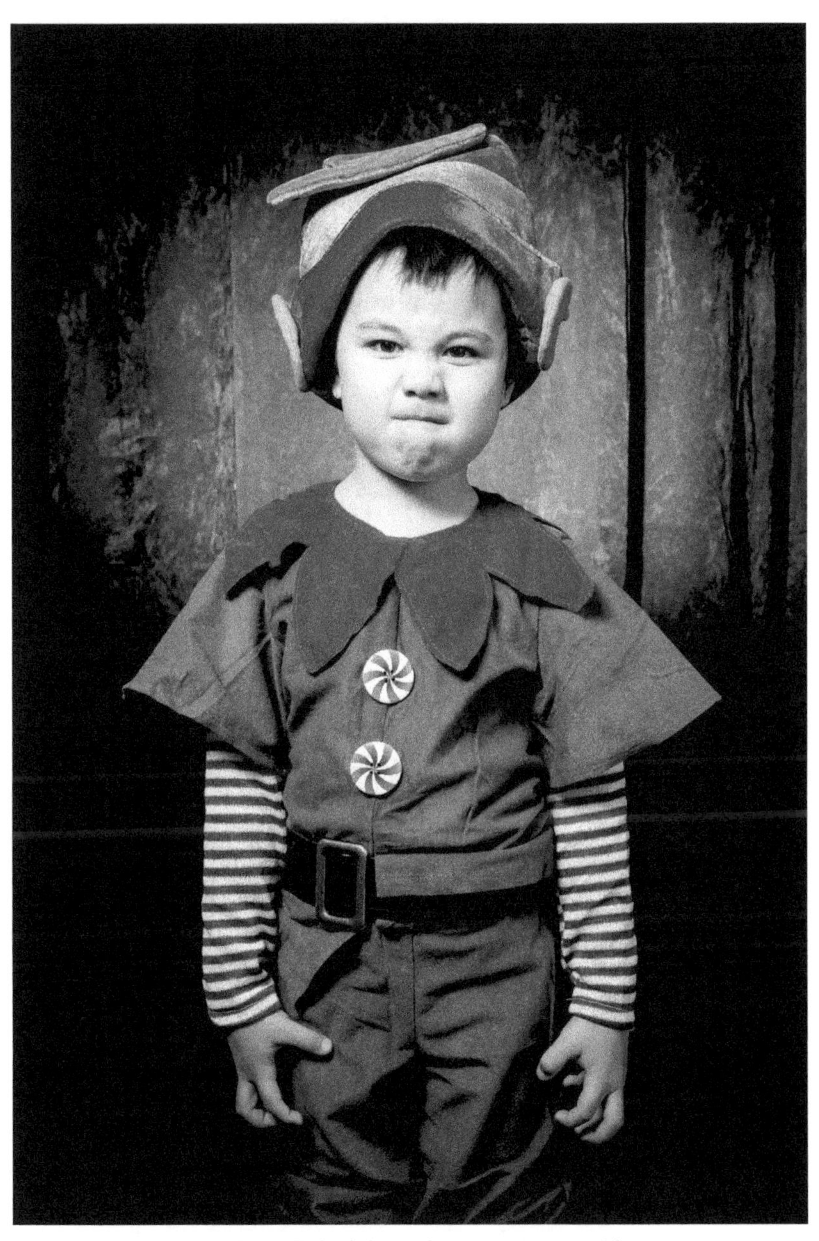

Arthur Cole (6) performs 'Angry Elf'

ANGRY ELF

A little ANGRY ELF enters.

Let me tell you something: I HATE being an ELF! Everyone looks down on me because I'm small and they make fun of my ears! Plus, I have to work in Santa's workshop all year, and I don't get paid. That is ILLEGAL! I'm going to the police! (*marches off making the woo-woo sound of a police car)*

NAUGHTY LIST

A SPOILT CHILD sits on Santa's lap.

I want a new iPhone. And a cover for it with puppies on, because I like puppies. And I want a puppy! But I don't want a dog so it needs to be the sort of dog that will look like a puppy forever. And an iPad. I've already got one, but I want a different colour. Rose gold. Are you getting all this? Perhaps you should write it down. Rose gold. The one I want is on Amazon. Do you have Amazon at the North Pole? Because I don't trust elves. Mum says you won't bring me presents if I don't tidy my room, but I know that's not true. She always gets me everything I want, otherwise I have tantrums and embarrass her in public. It's really funny. Everyone's staring like: 'Ooo what a bad kid!' and I'm like he-he… time for some presents! I shouldn't have to tidy my room anyway. I'm a kid, no one can force me into child labour! I know my rights. So anyway, Santa, don't forget anything on the list or I'll throw a BIG tantrum! Now smile for a selfie! (*beat*) Hey… why aren't you smiling?

SCROOGE

Adapted from A Christmas Carol, by Charles Dickens

Bah humbug! Will everyone PLEASE stop singing Christmas Carols? I'm trying to work in here! Capitalism doesn't stop for your stupid carols! But I can't concentrate because all I can hear is (*mimics*) 'Oh the first day of Christmas my bla bla bla bla blaaaaa' – what is this nonsense about partridges and turtle doves? It doesn't even make sense! (*mimicking*) Oh, here you go, I love you soooo much that I got you loads of birds to fly around and poop in your house! And by the way, there's now a huge pear tree in the living room. (*shouts*) Ridiculous! I hate Christmas! Bah humbug!

MARLEY'S GHOST

Adapted from A Christmas Carol, by Charles Dickens

(*In a ghostly way*) Scroooooge! Scrooooge! Behold, I am Marley's Ghost! I wear the chains I forged in life, created through my greed. No space of regret can make amends for the opportunities I misused! Tell me, Scrooge, why did I walk through crowds of my poor fellow beings with my eyes turned down? Were there no poor homes I might have visited? Scrooge, I am here tonight to warn you that you have a chance to escape my fate. You will be visited by three ghosts. Expect the first, when the bell tolls one!

THE NIGHT BEFORE CHRISTMAS

Adapted from A Visit from St. Nicholas

'Twas the night before Christmas,
when all through the house
Not a creature was stirring, not even a mouse!
The stockings were hung by the chimney with care,
In hopes that St. Nicholas soon would be there;
We children were nestled all snug in our beds;
While visions of sugar-plums danced in our heads!
When out on the lawn there arose such a clatter,
I sprang from my bed to see what was the matter.
Away to the window I flew like a flash,
Tore open the shutters and threw up the sash.
And what to my wondering eyes should appear?
But a miniature sleigh, and eight tiny reindeer!
With a little old driver, so lively and quick,
I knew in a moment it must be Saint Nick!
More rapid than eagles his reindeer they came,
And he whistled, and shouted, and called them by name!
'Now Dasher! Now, Dancer! Now, Prancer and Vixen!
On, Comet! On, Cupid! On Donner and Blitzen!'
His eyes-how they twinkled! His dimples how merry!
His cheeks were like roses, his nose like a cherry!
His kind little mouth was drawn up like a bow,
And the beard of his chin was as white as the snow!
He spoke not a word, but went straight to his work,
And filled all the stockings, then turned with a jerk.
And laying his finger aside of his nose,
And giving a nod, up the chimney he rose!
But I heard him exclaim, as he drove out of sight,
'Happy Christmas to all, and to all a good-night!'

DRAMA

MONSTER UNDER THE BED

(Drama)

(*Very afraid!*) I don't want to go to sleep because there's a monster under my bed! I'm not joking: it's a big, SCARY one! (*cries*) Mummy, I don't want to go to sleep in there! (*looks up*) But wait a minute... (*looks closely*) that's not a monster! That's just my teddy bear! Hi Teddy!

NO BIRTHDAY

(Drama)

I didn't get any birthday presents this year because I was naughty. I forgot to wash mummy's clothes. I forgot to make mummy's breakfast. I forgot to wake up mummy so she could go to work... so she didn't go to work. It's my fault. (*buries head in hands*) It's my fault. (*cries*) It's my fault.

SCHOOL BULLY

(Drama)

They took my lunch. Those kids over there. They said, 'give us your food, or we'll hit you.' So I gave them my cheese sandwiches and my apple. But I can't tell Daddy because he'll call me a wimp. He says I should fight back, but I don't want to fight back. I just want them to let me eat my lunch. But I guess, I'll have to stay hungry. (*rubs tummy*)

MOURNING GRANDPA

(Drama)

A YOUNG PERSON – in shock and grief.

Grandpa died last night. He was eighty-six. (*beat*) When I found out, I looked up at the sky and I couldn't believe it. Yesterday, he was whistling and making tea with that twinkle in his eye – how can all that just disappear? Where did his knowledge go? He knew everything about history and politics. And his smile… he always smiled when he told stories. Now I'll never hear him tell a story again… (*beat*) It makes me realise I'm going to die too, one day. All these thoughts in my head right now, all these things that seem so important; my feelings, my memories, my dreams – they'll be gone. And I keep— I keep thinking: I didn't visit him enough! I didn't ask him enough about his life and I have so many questions! Like, 'Why did he leave school when he was fourteen?', 'When did he first fall in love?', 'Did he have any regrets?' But I never asked. I just watched him make tea with that twinkle in his eye that I'll never see again. (*looks up at the sky*) I'm sorry, Grandpa. I hope the tea tastes good up there, and that you still whistle while you make it, and that your twinkling eyes are now stars.

FALSE START

(Drama)

A SWIMMER stands on the side of the pool, preparing to dive. The pre-dive movement is made in slow motion.

I've spent a year training for this. Every day at five AM and six PM. I've eaten the right foods and slept through school to be strong in the pool. For victory in this: the fifty metre freestyle. (*jumps*) No! No! A false start! I dived too soon. A split second too soon. I'm disqualified and it's all over. A whole year for nothing! I walk back to the changing room - the longest, saddest walk of my life. I hate everything right now. I hate the pool, I hate swimming, I hate all the people who ever encouraged me to want to do this. I'm never getting in a pool again! (*beat*) Then, I see this toddler walk by wearing arm bands, holding his mum's hand. I remember that was me, once. Me and Mum. I think of Mum and all the mornings she got out of the bed to drive me to swimming practice. All the nights she picked me up. All the hours she watched from the balcony. The next day, I get back in the pool.

THOUGHTFUL CHILD

(Drama)

A CHILD looks up from their iPad, takes off their glasses & says knowledgeably...

A high proportion of marriages end in divorce. My parents just got divorced, so I've been doing my research. I don't really understand because in movies when people get married, they promise they will stay together (*mimicking grandly*) 'until death do us part'... but neither of my parents are dead, so, it's a bit confusing. (*looks at iPad; reads*) 'According to the Government, 47% of divorces involve children under 18', (*looks up*) like me. It's not so bad though; I just stay at one house one week, and one house the next week, and that's fine. I mean, it's a bit annoying if I want to do band practice or sport on the weekends, because Dad doesn't want to take me to band practice and Mum doesn't want to take me to sport so... I always miss half of everything, (*reassuringly*) but that's fine. I know they love me. (*thoughtfully*) but then again... they used to love each other and now they don't, so... (*wide-eyed, fearful*) what if they divorce me one day?! They can't do that, right? I need to research if divorcing your child is a thing... (*looks worriedly at iPad and exits, searching for answers*)

SMALLTALK

(Comedy/Drama)

A YOUNG PERSON stands, unimpressed.

The only thing I hate more than going to the dentist, is going to the hairdressers. Going to the dentist is physically painful, so you can imagine how much I hate small talk. (*mimics a bubbly hairdresser with a big smile and over-energetic manner*) How ARE you? How's your day been? Any plans for the weekend? (*drops smile; then straight-faced – in a dry, adult way*) The mundane questions are endless. And always in the back of my mind, this thought: (*incredulously*) 'I don't know you! Why do you care? I'm just a kid and I'm only here because my mum thinks my fringe is too long so please stop asking me about school! I hate school. I hate small talk. And I hate hairdressers!' (*beat*) But then, in the silence I've created, I see her silently chopping and chopping and I think: WOW… that must be boring. Do her fingers hurt? Is she tired of standing? Is she glancing at the clock because she misses her kids? (*beat*) Maybe she just wants someone to talk to. Maybe it's been a long day, as long as school. So, in this weird moment, I get this crazy idea, and I say: (*sincerely*) 'How are you? How's your day been?' (*kindly*) 'Any plans for the weekend?'

MOVING SCHOOLS

(Drama)

A STUDENT on their first day at a new school.

Moving schools is hard. I should be used to it by now: my parents like moving. They're the 'grass is always greener on the other side' type. So, a new teacher. New timetable. New classroom. New uniform. New rules. The first problem is that everyone's already friends – divided into groups. Usually, you fall in with the unpopular loners, then someone mid-ranking will walk up and say, 'No, you don't want to hang out with them.' The accent is different. Sometimes, you use a word from home and everyone looks at you funny, and you want to shout, 'Yeah, there are thousands of languages and dialects, so yes I do use a different word for that object, ignorant child who has never left their home town!' But… saying that doesn't help you make friends. So you just start using the new word. Eventually, it gets easier. You find a group, or at least one good friend. Then, Mum and Dad decide to move again. And I'm back to square one. My first day at school.

DETERMINED DANCER

(Drama)

A DANCER tries to do a pirouette - but falls. She grimaces – it hurts – but she picks herself up with determination, and tries again. She falls. She screams in a mixture of pain and frustration, then looks up.*

I always wanted to be a dancer. I begged mum to send me when I was four. (*nostalgically*) The older girls had these beautiful dance costumes and I wanted one so bad! I wanted to be like them. To have my hair tied back in a bun. To look graceful. To dance and make everyone proud! (*beat*) Now my feet are bleeding and my knees are bruised and this morning— (*struggling, emotional*) this morning, the dance teacher walked up to me, looked me in the eye, and said: (*coldly; becoming the teacher*) 'You're not good enough. You will never be a professional dancer. Go home. Give up.' So, I decided to give up... but then I got angry, really angry, and by dinner time I'd given up on giving up because you know what? Dancing makes me happy! When I dance, I feel strong, and powerful, and free. (*with strength and attitude*) So, if that bitter old bat thinks she can tell me to go home and give up, she's got another thing coming! She better get used to seeing my stubborn face at dance class, because I'm a dancer, and I will never give up! (*She does a pirouette again, and falls. She does a pirouette again... and it's perfect. She smiles triumphantly.)*

** or any dance move that fits the dance experience of the performer.*

READING ALOUD

(Drama)

A YOUNG PERSON stands holding an open book.

Miss Smith says, 'Please stand and read aloud.' The whole class goes quiet. I can feel them all tensing up, looking at each other, or looking down. They want to say something, but what can they say? It's not Miss Smith's fault. She's new and she doesn't know. She sees me: tall for my age, well-spoken, attentive, and thinks: yes, a good example for the class. (*looks at book*) I look at the words and they look like meaningless squiggles that turn into faces that laugh at me for being so stupid. I think I can make out the first word – 'The' – but then the second word could be anything. It starts with 'R'; 'Rabbit'? 'Raisin'? 'Random'? I'm not even reading, I'm just trying to think of every word I know that starts with 'R'. Miss Smith is staring, looking kind of horrified and sorry. Like she should have been told. At lunchtime, she's going to go to the staffroom and say, 'Did you know that student can't read?' And the other teachers will say, 'We know. That one comes from a troubled home. Sad story. Do you want to hear it?' And Miss Smith will never ask me to read aloud again.

PICKED LAST

(Drama)

A STUDENT stands in sports clothes, arms folded in the cold.

Picked last. Again. Can't blame them; I'm terrible at football, and netball, and basketball, and dodgeball, and baseball, and handball and you guessed it: any sport involving a ball. It's fascinating how they get so passionate about who has the ball and what happens to the ball. I zone out: I think about homework, or what I'm having for dinner, or the way the clouds (*looks up*) look like certain shapes. That cloud looks like a bunny rabbit, eating a small crocodile… holding a flower. (*jumps*) Ahhh! Someone's shouting at me! (*mimics gruff sportsperson shouting*) 'Pay attention, left wing!' What's left wing? Am I left wing?! (*moves awkwardly*) I fumble and make no contact with the ball whatsoever. Everyone groans. I think about the library, and the smell of books. The smell of books is actually the smell of pages decaying. Decay smells good. Are we still playing? Apparently, yes, but they're desperate to bench me. I hope I get benched. I want to sit on that bench so bad. The game ends. We lose. In the changing rooms, everyone talks about how bad I messed up that pass. I wish I knew what a pass was. The hot water in the shower feels good: warm, like nothing really matters. After dinner, I sit and read a book, and forget all about the game and the ball and the changing room… and the bruises.

GUARDIAN ANGEL

(Drama)

The YOUNG PERSON peers through binoculars.

Six PM. They always have dinner at six PM. Just the four of them: Mum, Dad, Katie and Joey. Mum always cooks vegetables and Joey isn't allowed ice cream until he's eaten every last one. (*fondly*) He pulls the cutest faces when he eats carrots. And Katie always has her stuffed giraffe at the table... (*looking through binoculars, excitedly*) Look, there he is: Hi Giraffy! After dinner they walk through that door right there; I don't know where it goes, but (*with subtle longing*) I imagine they read bedtime stories and fall asleep so happy. (*lowers the binoculars*)

(*Suddenly paranoid*) You won't tell anyone you saw me spying, will you? The kids in the home call me weird, but I can't help but notice them having dinner… through my long distance binoculars. (*thoughtfully*) Look, maybe the 24 hour surveillance is a bit weird, but I need to know where they are at all times. Just in case. (*becoming panicked*) Because— because what if mum and dad don't come home, and there's no one to make dinner for Katie and Joey? They don't know how to look after themselves, so it will be up to me. Because I'm the oldest… (*Realises they have confused two realities. A beat.*)

The kids in the home call me weird. They call me weird because I don't really know the names of those kids I watch through my binoculars. The boy with the carrots, the girl with the giraffe… I named them after my brother and sister.

Katie and Joey were babies, so they got rehomed. (*Resentfully*) Foster parents want them young so they don't remember all the horrible things that happened before. I was too old to forget.

So I've decided, I'm going to watch over those kids like a guardian angel, and then maybe someone will be a guardian angel for Katie and Joey, and make sure their foster parents give them stuffed toys and bedtime stories.

(*Upset*) Like I should have. I should have protected them! I should have watched them 24 hours a day. Because I'm the oldest. (*head in hands, guilt-ridden*) I'm the oldest, I'm the oldest. I'm the oldest. (*breathes, then lifts binoculars and continues watching*)

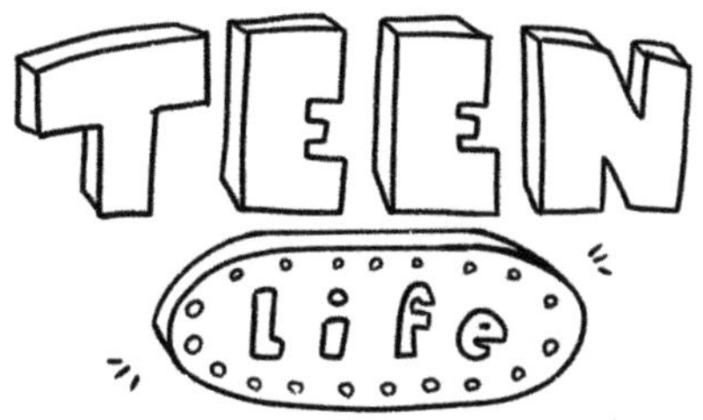
TEEN
Life

Elodie Khan (14) performs 'The Break Up'

MODERN ROMEO

(Comedy)

(*In a romantic way*) But soft! What light through yonder window breaks? It is the East, and Juliet is the sun! Arise, fair sun, and kill the envious moon, Who is already sick and pale with grief, That thou her maid art — (*makes a frightened squeal and hides in a ball; when he speaks next, his persona has changed to something quite modern*) I think she saw me. Is this weird, hiding outside a thirteen-year-old girl's bedroom in the dark? I really like her, you know, and I'm new to this romance thing so I thought: who better to learn from than Romeo? So, I snuck into her parent's party tonight disguised in a Halloween mask, (*pulls out scary Halloween mask to show audience*) and now I'm hiding in a bush, declaring my love in iambic pentameter! It worked for Romeo. I think her parents are going to love me. Wait. (*beat*) What's that sound? Is that… is that a siren? (*runs away*)

INDEPENDENT

(Comedy)

I moved out of home six weeks ago. I've been eating pasta with tomato sauce ever since. It was the only meal I knew how to make. I eat pasta before I do assignments because I need the energy. I eat pasta during assignments because I need something to keep me going. I eat pasta after assignments as a reward. I'm basically a giant carb. So today, I went to a gym for the first time. I worked out on the treadmill for thirty minutes, then I rowed, then I worked my core, then I did weights. I felt so proud of myself that I came home and ate a cheesy pasta bake. It was delicious: full of cheesy, mouth-watering guilt. Then, I called Mum and asked her something I never thought I'd ask: 'Mum, how do you make a salad?'

THE BREAK UP

(Comedy)

A TEENAGER looks at her phone; her eyes widen in horror.

He broke up with me! I can't believe it. He. Broke up. With me. (*distraught*) Oh my goddddddddd, whyyyyyyyyy. My life is over! I'll never meet anyone as nice as him ever again! He was SO romantic, like the most romantic guy you've ever met. He used to send the sweetest Snapchats. He'd stand in front of the mirror at the gym and flex his muscles and write, (*mimics his voice*) 'You're a lucky girl'. (*sincerely, distraught again*) I was so lucky! And once, he mentioned me in his Instagram story! He was eating pizza and playing Xbox with his friends, and he wrote, 'babe, I'm really busy so I can't meet your parents.' Hashtag 'soz'. It was so sweet he took the time to let me know! And once – once – he sent me flowers (*nods, recalling*)... I've never seen so many beautiful flower emojis in my life. And now, it's all over. (*distraught*) I'll never find love as special as that ever again! Break ups are soooo hard! I guess there's nothing I can do but... (*takes phone, blocks him*) block him on social media. (*sighs, instantly cheers up*) Ahhh, that's better. (*scrolls*) Wait, who is that? That guy is hot! I think I'm in love... (*wanders off checking out new guy's pics*)

THE BIGGEST PARTY OF THE YEAR

(Comedy)

A TEENAGER wears a sweater over party clothes.

(*Excitedly*) Tonight, this girl at school is having the biggest party of the year. And guess what? (*smile drops*) I'm not allowed to go. Apparently, I have to stay home because my aunts, uncles and cousins are visiting from interstate. I have to spend New Year's Eve talking to people I don't like just because we're related. Mum and Dad are like: (*mimics*) 'It's just a party! Our family only gets together once a year and you won't be a kid much longer' – excuse me, I'm not a kid – 'so, you need to spend time with the family while you have the chance!' That's exactly why I need to go to the party! Because family never goes away – I'm stuck with you for the rest of my life! But these friends and this party – that's not going to last forever. And it's not JUST a party. For the next few months at school, everyone's going to be saying, 'Do you remember that time at the New Year's party when that really funny thing happened?' and everyone will be like, 'Oh my god, that was so funny!' except me, because I'll be stood there remembering how I spent the night talking to my weird Aunty Jean about her collection of Russian dolls. Or Uncle Matthew, who believes that everything is a conspiracy and will spend at least two hours talking about how the flag was moving in the photograph of the moon landing! Well, guess what. I've got Uber installed on my phone, and I'm not afraid to use it. (*takes off sweater to reveal party outfit underneath*) At precisely ten PM, when Aunty Jean is snoring on the sofa, I'll be gone. And when they ask: where did you go? I'll say: 'I went to the bathroom. For three hours. And it was awesome.'

THINGS I HATE
(Comedy/Drama)

A TEENAGER enters holding a list – deadpan, almost bored.

Here is a list of things I hate. (*consults list*) I hate exams, and essays, and the font Times New Roman, size twelve. I hate people who don't stand to the side on the escalator. I hate it when you order a hot chocolate and it's served lukewarm. I hate how retail workers are helpful when you're just browsing, but disappear when you actually need help. I hate people who walk slowly. I hate crying babies on aeroplanes. (*thinks*) Actually, that's mean. (*takes a pencil and adds a couple of words, then re-reads*). I hate the parents of crying babies on aeroplanes. I hate it when people don't look like their profile photos. I hate how hard it is to be authentic when everyone's pretending. I hate free apps with in-app purchases. I hate reality TV. I hate Pop Idol and X Factor and The Voice and So You Think You Can Dance and Dancing with the Stars and Dancing on Ice and any other TV talent show that celebrates the fact that talent is common and reward is rare. I hate it when my laptop runs out of battery. I hate how I'm dying slowly, every day, and I can't stop it. I hate when the writing on a T-shirt fades after one wash. I hate how I'm going to lose everyone I love, eventually. And finally, I hate it when psychologists make me articulate my feelings by writing lists of things that I hate. It's really unhelpful and look! I got a paper cut… (*writes on paper, then reads*) I hate paper cuts.

EXAM STRESS

(Comedy)

A sleep-deprived TEENAGER, hyped up on energy drinks.

I have an exam tomorrow, except I stayed up all night to study so it's more accurate to say, I have an exam in two hours. It's dawn, the birds are chirping in the trees, oblivious to the headache I have from downing too many energy drinks and trying to memorise all of the American Presidents who served during the Cold War. (*reciting fast*) Harry Truman 45-53. Dwight Eisenhower 53-61. John Kennedy 61-63; he's the one who got shot on the Grassy Knoll – what the hell is a knoll? I don't know. Lyndon Johnson 63-69. Richard Nixon 69-74. Then Ford until 77, Carter until 81 and Reagan until 89 when the Berlin Wall fell. BAM! Take that history teacher. Now, the Russian ones: Khrushchev… um… Khrushchev— oh my god, who were the others?! I'm going to fail. The Cold War, by the way, is the dumbest thing. It's literally a war where nothing happened. WHY DO THEY THINK WE NEED TO KNOW THIS? I could be doing something useful with my life, OK? I could be designing an app or being an entrepreneur or founding the next Facebook but here I am memorising Cold War 101: Men Being Suspicious and Stuff. I'm going to bed. (*goes to sleep, then calls out*) Nooooo, Mum, just five more minutes!

TEEN PUNK

(Comedy)

A TEEN PUNK enters.

You know what sucks? Living in a time when nothing I like is cool. Being surrounded by princesses who listen to Taylor Swift and spend all day on Instagram taking 'candid' photos. Why couldn't I have grown up in a cooler time? Anywhere in the 80s, 90s or early 2000s. The age of punk rock. Guitars. Mohawks. Eyeliner. Piercings everywhere! Nirvana. Blink 182. Greenday. If I show an interest in any of that, everyone at school looks at me like I'm weird. But seriously, is it just me, or does all the music on the radio today sound the same? I know that makes me sound like someone's grandmother, but it's true. And technology! Man, it must have been amazing to have a phone and all it did was call! When you couldn't browse or follow and you didn't have to maintain six social media accounts. So peaceful. I was clearly born in the wrong time. If anyone invents a time machine, let me know. Like "Back to the Future"! See, even the movies were better. We've got CGI and every special effect you can think of, but we can't tell a story. If I have to see one more Disney remake or Avengers sequel, I'm going to die. But I guess I can't do much about it, so I'll do what any good punk would do: listen to music and quietly hate everyone. (*puts on headphones and sings Blink 182's 'All the Small Things'*)

TRYING ON CLOTHES

(Drama)

A TEENAGER, dressed in plain, comfortable clothes, holds up two uncomfortable-looking, girly dresses.

I hate shopping for clothes. My Mum makes me do it (*mimics*) 'Let's go buy you some trendy new clothes to smarten you up!' She's out there now, waiting for me. I better hurry up or she'll come in here and start being that embarrassing mum everyone overhears in the changing rooms. The mum who wants her daughter to look a certain way. The mum who doesn't know how to make her daughter feel better about herself. The mum who thinks clothes are the answer. (*picks up dress; holds it up against herself*) Does this define me, mum? Will this make me happy, mum? (*puts dress down*) I don't get that rush that most people get when they buy clothes, because I know it's all a lie. All the advertisements that try to make us feel like we need to buy the latest fashion. We don't! There's nothing wrong with my dress from last year. It's a waste of money, and material, and time, for what? So that people who own department stores can get rich? So I can fit in at school? (*struggling to contain emotion*) So that my mum won't get embarrassed by me at parties, when she points across the room, looks me up and down without smiling, and says, 'That's my daughter.' (*picks up clothes*) Sorry mum, it's not happening. (*exits*)

POPULAR GIRL

(Drama)

The POPULAR GIRL looks up from her phone.

I'm the most popular girl in school. I'm not showing off: it's a fact. My parents are rich so I have the best clothes, the best house, the best parties. (*beat*) But no one cares if I have the best personality, the best grades... the best mental health. All that matters is how I look on the outside. On the outside, I wear cute skirts and high heels and everyone says, 'Where did you get that? I'm SO jealous!' (*beat*) But my feet hurt and the cute skirts make me feel sick when I look in the mirror. On the outside, my makeup looks perfect, but I have to wear three layer of concealer to hide the circles under my eyes. I'm tired. I'm so tired. On the outside, my hair looks shiny – but the hair clips cover bald patches from where I've pulled it out. On the outside, I'm confident, but inside I'm scared all the time. Scared of what will happen one day when I have to grow up and get a job… I'm not smart, or talented, like other kids. The kids I'm too cool to hang out with. I'm jealous of them! I wish I could stay home. I wish I could just sit and read a book. But I have to go to parties. I have to get compliments. I have to post to Instagram three times a day. I have to be the popular girl because if I'm not… all that's left is what's on the inside. (*resolutely*) And I can't let anyone see that.

SANDCASTLES

(Comedy)

A TEENAGER enters, reluctantly dressed for the beach.

I don't want to be here; my family made me come. I hate the beach. Nothing but expensive ice cream, hot sand that burns your feet, tourists, skin cancer and sharks. Oh, and a toddler peeing in the sea right next to me, up against my leg like he's a dog and I'm a lamppost. And don't get me started on the bodies. All the flat stomachs and abs are making me want to cry, and then comfort myself with food. When I see bodies like this in magazines, I always tell myself they're photoshopped, like: 'That's unrealistic! People don't really look like that!' Then I come to the beach and I realise: nope, I'm just ugly. (*looks out at the audience with resentment*) Look at them, smiling with their perfect teeth (*mimics*) 'Oh look at me! Look at my abs! Look at my designer beach towel! I wear sea salt spray in my hair even though I'm literally stood next to the sea!' (*beat*) All I've got is Mum's Coles brand Factor 50 and a SpongeBob towel I've had since primary school. Yep, it's like school all over again, and I'm still a pasty loser. Well, guess what's more important than being an Instagram clone? Being happy. So, I'm going to build the most amazing sandcastle they've ever seen! Then we'll see who's jealous.

CYBER BULLY

(Drama)

The VICTIM of a cyber bully.

The first message made fun of my profile photo: (*mimics*) 'You look so uncomfortable in that photo! Haha.' I changed the photo. Then a laughing emoji. I changed it again. The messages got worse: (*mimics*) 'Your skin is horrible. Your hair is greasy. You're fat. You look so stupid when you try to answer questions in class. Everyone knows you don't understand anything. Stupid AND ugly; your parents must be so proud.' I was too scared to block them. I was embarrassed to show Mum and Dad… they thought I was happy. They thought I had friends. The messages came all night, until three or four AM. I felt my heart drop to my stomach every time. I said, 'Please stop! Please!' Laughing emoji. 'Please stop!' A GIF of a school kid getting slapped. Over and over. A GIF with a scene from a horror movie where someone is being followed. A GIF of a grave. My grave. I didn't go to school. I pretended I was sick for three weeks. I checked the wardrobe before I went to bed. I dreamt they were standing at the window, laughing, and then SMASH. I saw my blood. SMASH. I saw my grave. I saw them standing over it, and the 'ding-ding' of a new message. Laughing emoji. Laughing emoji. Laughing emoji.

BABY SISTER

(Comedy/Drama)

A 16-year-old stands, full of resentment.

So, my parents decided to have another baby. There's a sixteen year age gap – like, seriously? She's going to think I'm her aunt! How could mum and dad think this was a good idea? I can't believe they even still… (*tries not to think about it*). Around the baby, they act like perfect parents. Dad is humming nursery rhymes and taking her to the zoo and (*mystified*) being nice, and I'm like: who are you? Are you the same dad who spent the last sixteen years shouting at me? And Mum – Mum lives next to the high chair getting excited every time the baby makes a weird noise that sounds vaguely like a word. It's clearly not a word! While I'm here just watching, like a ghost who lives in the attic, occasionally haunting my parents for attention. (*beat*) For most of my life, I was an only child. People used to say 'Aren't you lonely?' Um, no! It was awesome. 100% of the family resources were allocated to me. Now it's all like, 'Ohhh finances are stretched. Ohhh, nappies are expensive.' I feel betrayed. They spoil her all the time; her three-month wardrobe is bigger than mine. It's like when old people become grandparents and try to make up for all their parenting mistakes by being the best grandparents ever but because mum and dad are so old, they're just doing it now! With me, it was all strict bedtimes and chores and (*mimics*) 'we're not angry, we're just disappointed.' But with her, they have another chance. (*a concealed pain reveals itself*) I don't mind the nappies or the crying or the pointless trips to the zoo. What hurts is that it feels like… it feels like she's here because they failed with me, but this time, they're going to get it right.

MELODRAMATIC EXPLORER

(Comedy)

An EXPLORER emerges, panting. She fumbles to open a bottle of water and holds it over her tongue. It's empty.

(*A scream of rage*) Arrgggghhhhhhh! (*throws the bottle*) I HATE Bear Grylls! If you don't know who he is, he's the reason my tongue is swollen and I've got mosquito bites in every orifice and my idiot boyfriend is getting DUMPED as soon as I get out of this stupid desert!

(*Mimicking*) 'Let's go exploring! We can be like Bear Grylls on his survival show, where he makes shelter from leaves and gets water from bamboo!' It took an hour for me to realise he was basing all of his survival knowledge on an episode set in the Amazon. I think (*mimics*) 'let's find a river, but watch out for piranhas and pink dolphins' was the giveaway.

So, where is he now? Well, he decided to be a hero and go and look for help. What. An. Idiot. Everyone knows the first rule is to stick together, because then you can help each other find food, and if you can't find food, then you can eat the weaker person.

FINE. I'm a strong, independent woman. I can take care of myself. It'll be getting dark soon. Step one: build a fire. (*looks around, picks up sticks*) How hard can it be? (*tries rubbing sticks together; tries harder; then has a meltdown*) Arrgggghhhhhhh! I only got these nails done last week! (*ugly crying*) And this polish is supposed to last three weeks! And I'll be dead by then anywayyyy! (*sinks dramatically to the floor; then, pathetically)* The sand is hot. *(suddenly stands up with a brilliant idea*) Oh my god, I could shoot a flare! They would see it for miles! (*smile drops*) I don't have a flare gun.

(*Laments, then suddenly sees something in the distance*) Wait? What's that? It can't be… is it a mirage? (*looks closely; then with candid certainty*) No, that's a Seven Eleven. (*looks awkwardly at the audience*) Don't judge me, OK. The sand dunes at the beach are pretty intense. (*awkwardly picks up discarded water bottle, then with forced dignity)* Littering is bad. *(exits)*

SOCIA MEDIA SUSHI

(Drama)

My next door neighbour has 2500 Instagram followers. She's six. And I know her mum runs her account and that's pretty messed up, but sometimes I wish my parents had been that forward-thinking. (*shows the selfie to the audience*) Pretty nice, huh? You may laugh, but taking selfies is hard work. The right lighting, the right look – the right caption that seems totally spontaneous even though it took three hours. I put more thought into this selfie than any school assignment I've ever done. Who cares about school? Someone my age has ten million followers. Someone my age is lying on a beach living their perfect, sponsored life. Someone my age has just launched their own reality TV series. Someone my age just became the world's youngest self-made millionaire. I might as well just give up! Because getting an A in English or looking somewhat good in my school uniform is never going to compare to that. I'm average and I'll always be average and what's the point in an average life? I'll never be a big fish. Not even a big fish in a small pond. Just a tiny, tiny fish like a krill or something. So small, no one notices and then a whale eats you. But maybe that's not so bad, because the pretty fish get carved up and served up on a platter. That's what Instagram is: a sushi carousel with everyone's smiles and filtered lives just spinning around and around being dissected and I feel like I'm drowning (*overwhelmed*) I feel like I'm drowning I feel like I'm drowning I feel like I'm drowning I feel like I'm drowning I feel like I'm drowning I feel like I'm— (*Silence; a few deep breaths*) I'm just really tired. (*Holds the phone up and represses everything in order to give a fake smile).*

SCAR

(Comedy/Drama)

You know when someone insults you while they're pretending to be your best friend? Jessica starts conversationally clawing me and I can see it happening like that moment in the Lion King when Scar reaches out to pull Mufasa from the ledge, then digs in his claws.

And I'm like, 'Hey Jessica, your blonde hair extensions can't hide your black soul. These people may think you're hot, but isn't it ironic that you love taking photos of yourself because you hate yourself? Looking through your Instagram is like X-raying the Mona Lisa and seeing The Scream.' She doesn't get the art reference.

Then my mum arrives to pick me up. Yeah, my mum picks me up from parties at 10 PM because I'm a loser. She's like, 'Hi baby, how was the party? Did you and Jessica make friends?' I'm like, 'No, Mum, Jessica is evil.' She's like, 'Don't talk about your sister like that!' Then Jessica gets in the car. (*Imitates Jessic*a) 'Oh my god, Mum, can you not make me take her to parties? It's like, so embarrassing.'

'Stop exaggerating Jessica! All I did was tell everyone how insecure you are. That's not a lie, unlike your face. I'm sorry you hate yourself but the truth is better than your Barbie extensions and fake eyelashes, which are coming unglued by the way, so just shut up!'

Jessica starts crying, and then she vomits on the floor of the car. (*beat*) I'm not sure why I feel bad then. Maybe it's because I didn't hold back her hair and now her blonde extensions are brown… the colour her hair used to be, when she was my little sister; or because she's looking into the pool of vomit and realising she's not in love with her reflection. I wish she could find a clear pool of water somewhere and look beyond the surface, because deep down… she's beautiful.

I put my hand on her shoulder and I say, 'Jessica, the truth is: I'm the Scar to your Mufasa. You'll always be the golden child in this family and I have to live with that, but I'll try to be nicer to you from now on, and resist the temptation to… throw you into a stampede of antelope.'

She stops crying, and we stay up all night watching The Lion King.

ALMOST 20

(Drama/Comedy)

This is my last day on earth as a teenager, because at midnight tonight: I turn twenty.

And I am NOT OK with that. So, I've decided to start a protest: (*pulls out a sign that says 'DOWN WITH MORTALITY'*). My parents are even more concerned than when I went on climate strike.

They say, 'Don't be silly! You're so young! You've got your whole life ahead of you!' You can't fool me. I know it's a slippery slope. Twenty leads to thirty and thirty leads to forty and forty leads to death. (*puts down sign, a little sadly*)

My parents always sigh when they look in the bathroom mirror, pulling apart the crows feet at the corners of their eyes while wondering where the years went. But I don't need wrinkles to realise time flies. I was in year seven yesterday. Year four the day before. The day before that I rode a bike for the first time.

Now, my friends have moved away to go to university or get jobs or travel and nothing's like it used to be. We used to always go to the movies on Wednesdays. We used to go on bike rides next to the river. We used to make fun of the evil French teacher at school.

We used to have sleepovers and watch scary films we weren't allowed to watch, and shout until our parents came down and said, (*mimics grumpy parents*) 'Keep it down; we've got work in the morning!'

Now, we can stay up as late as we want and watch anything we want, but it's not the same.

Alone, in our different cities; in tiny rooms, we hide from assignments or jobs or ourselves – in front of the TV at three AM, streaming TV shows for hours and hours, wondering what the hell we're going to do with our lives when the current season ends.

In the morning, I'll go to a horrible part-time job with a horrible manager and there's nothing I can do about it because apparently when you're an adult you just have to put up with it. And I can't quit because now the phone bill is in my name! And I can't live without my phone because I need it to compare my life to the lives of my more successful friends.

It isn't fair! Getting a year older every year isn't fair. I don't want to get old. I don't want to get married and have children around the same time that I give up on my dreams, then drive my kids around to ballet practice and sport and complain about how stressful having kids is, until I'm finally stood sighing as I look in the bathroom mirror, being watched by the miserable teenager I brought into the world.

(*Picks up the sign*) I'm not scared of wrinkles. I'm not even scared of death. I'm scared because I know life is never going to be that good again. And my twentieth birthday, it's just the beginning of *(spins sign around to reveal: 'THE END')* The End.

classic characters from LITERATURE

PETER PAN

Adapted from Peter Pan, by J.M. Barrie

(*Waking up and looking around the room*) Who is that? (*fixes eyes on a spot on the ground*) Oh, it's you, Tinkerbell! (*listening*) What's that? Wendy and the boys have been captured by pirates?! I'll rescue them! Let's go... (*starts to leave, then stops and looks worriedly at Tinkerbell. He picks up an empty bottle of medicine from the floor.*) Why, Tink, you have drunk my medicine! It was poisoned, and you drank it to save my life! Tink, dear Tink, are you dying? (*speaks now to the audience*) Her light is growing faint, and if it goes out, that means she is dead! Her voice is so low I can't tell what she is saying. She says—she says she thinks she could get well again if children believed in fairies! (*passionately to the audience*) Do you believe in fairies? Say quick that you believe! If you believe, clap your hands! (*the audience clap, and Tinkerbell is saved*) Oh, thank you, thank you, thank you! And now to rescue Wendy!

WENDY

Adapted from Peter Pan, by J.M. Barrie

Oh, hello! Would you like to hear a story? It's rather exciting. Well, I was sleeping in my bedroom when I heard a strange sound. I sat up in bed, and saw a boy crying on the floor! I said, 'Why are you crying?' and he said, 'I've lost my shadow' and I said, 'I don't think that's possible', but then I saw his shadow running all over the ceiling in a very naughty way! The boy said his name was Peter Pan. I asked him where he lived and he said, 'Second star to the right, and then straight on till morning!' and I said, 'That's a funny address. Is that where you send the letters?' and he said, 'Don't get letters' and I said, 'Your mother must get letters?' and he said, 'I don't have a mother.' No mother? How terrible! So I jumped up, caught his shadow, and I sewed it back on! He had been trying to stick it back on with soap. Boys. Then, a rather grumpy fairy called Tinkerbell appeared. But THAT is another story.

OLIVER TWIST

Adapted from Oliver Twist, by Charles Dickens

The Workhouse was an awful place! Imagine it: a hundred hungry orphans working day in, day out. They dreamed of food, glorious food, but all they had was one bowl of gruel per day. Have you ever had gruel? It's like porridge, but thinner. One day, the big boy Fred told everyone that if he didn't get more food, he would eat the small boy who slept next to him. He was joking, but the children were so scared that they decided someone must go to the master and ask for more food. And who do you think drew the short straw? That's right: me. Oliver Twist. So the next day, at dinnertime, I walked (*walk, acting out the words*) slowly, shaking, to the master, and in a fearful voice, I said, 'Please, sir... I want some more.'

ARTFUL DODGER

Adapted from Oliver Twist, by Charles Dickens

Oh, 'ello! Goin' to London? Got any lodgings? Money? Well, don't fret your eyelids on that score. Stick with me. They call me the Artful Dodger on account of me being so artful. I've got to be in London tonight; and I know a 'spectable old gentleman as lives there, wot'll give you lodgings for nothink, and never ask for the change—that is, if any genelman he knows interduces you. Follow me, Oliver Twist!

PIP

From Great Expectations, by Charles Dickens

Out of my thoughts! Estella, you are part of my existence, part of myself. You have been in every line I have ever read, since I first came here, the rough common boy whose poor heart you wounded even then. You have been in every prospect I have ever seen since – on the river, on the sails of the ships, on the marshes, in the clouds, in the light, in the darkness, in the wind, in the woods, in the sea, in the streets. You have been the embodiment of every graceful fancy that my mind has ever become acquainted with. The stones of which the strongest London buildings are made, are not more real, or more impossible to displace with your hands, than your presence and influence have been to me, there and everywhere, and will be. Estella, to the last hour of my life, you cannot choose but remain part of my character, part of the little good in me, part of the evil. But, in this separation I associate you only with the good, and I will faithfully hold you to that always, for you must have done me far more good than harm, let me feel now what sharp distress I may. O God bless you, God forgive you!

DICKENSIAN NARRATOR

Adapted from A Tale of Two Cities, by Charles Dickens

It was the best of times, it was the worst of times, it was the age of wisdom, it was the age of foolishness, it was the epoch of belief, it was the epoch of incredulity, it was the season of Light, it was the season of Darkness, it was the spring of hope, it was the winter of despair, we had everything before us, we had nothing before us, we were all going directly to Heaven, we were all going directly the other way. There was a king with a large jaw and a queen with a plain face, on the throne of England; there was a king with a large jaw and a queen with a fair face, on the throne of France. In both countries it was clearer than crystal to the lords of the State preserves of loaves and fishes, that things in general were settled for ever.

ELIZABETH BENNET

Adapted from Pride and Prejudice, by Jane Austen

In marrying your nephew, I should not consider myself as quitting that sphere. He is a gentleman; I am a gentleman's daughter; so far we are equal. Your ladyship wants Mr. Darcy to marry your daughter; but would my giving you the wished-for promise make their marriage at all more probable? Allow me to say, Lady Catherine, that the arguments with which you have supported this extraordinary application have been as frivolous as the application was ill-judged. You have widely mistaken my character, if you think I can be worked on by such persuasions as these. How far your nephew might approve of your interference in his affairs, I cannot tell; but you have certainly no right to concern yourself in mine. I must beg, therefore, to be importuned no further on the subject!

MR DARCY

Adapted from Pride and Prejudice, by Jane Austen

I have been a selfish being all my life, in practice, though not in principle. As a child I was taught what was right, but I was not taught to correct my temper. I was given good principles, but left to follow them in pride and conceit. As an only son, I was spoilt by my parents, who allowed, encouraged, almost taught me to be selfish and overbearing; to care for none beyond my own family circle; to think meanly of all the rest of the world; to wish at least to think meanly of their sense and worth compared with my own. Such I was, from eight to twenty-eight; and such I might still have been but for you, dearest, loveliest Elizabeth! You taught me a lesson, hard indeed at first, but most advantageous. You showed me how insufficient were all my pretensions to please a woman worthy of being pleased.

JO MARCH

Adapted from Little Women, by Louisa May Alcott

I think that families are the most beautiful things in the world! I love my family dearly. Society, however… They say, 'Jo, you must stop being wild! Give up this writing nonsense and find yourself a husband!' No thank you! Every family has an old spinster, and I mean to be the spinster in this family! That's what I thought, until I met Professor Bhaer. He had the kindest eyes I ever saw and more books than I could count. I didn't have to hide my opinions or my wildness. Bhaer had a friend who said, 'Well, yes, women ought to be able to vote because they're good!' And I said, 'I find it poor logic to say that because women are good, women should vote. Men do not vote because they are good; they vote because they are male, and women should vote, not because we are good but because we are human beings and citizens of this country.' Bhaer looked at me and I knew I had found a man who wasn't afraid of a strong woman. Perhaps I won't be an old maid after all.

JANE EYRE

Adapted from Jane Eyre, by Charlotte Brontë

Mr Rochester, I have seen Miss Ingram; a noble and beautiful woman — your bride. So I tell you I must go! Do you think I can stay to become nothing to you? Do you think I am a machine — without feelings? Do you think, because I am poor, obscure, plain, and little, I am soulless and heartless? You think wrong! I have as much soul as you, and as much heart! And if God had gifted me with some beauty and wealth, I should have made it as hard for you to leave me, as it is now for me to leave you. I am not talking to you now through the medium of custom, conventionalities, nor even of mortal flesh; it is my spirit that addresses your spirit; just as if both had passed through the grave, and we stood at God's feet, equal — as we are!

HISTORICAL
figures

JULIUS CAESAR

Based on the life of Julius Caesar

The difference between a republic and an empire is the loyalty of one's army. Hi, I'm Julius Caesar. You may remember me as the army commander who crossed the Rubicon – that's a river – into Roman Italy and took over Rome! Now I'm the boss around here. Everyone does what I say – it's awesome! For example, the other day I was feeling random, so I said, 'Let's change the calendar!' And they were like: (*uncertainly*) 'Uhh, O-OK.' (*confiding in the audience*) I've got an amazing idea for the name of the seventh month, but that will have to wait. I've got a meeting with the senate now. I'm not looking forward to it; the senators have been really moody lately, and Brutus has been acting pretty shifty. (*looks at watch*) The 15th of March. I have a feeling this is going to be a long day.

QUEEN ELIZABETH I

Adapted from Elizabeth's Tilbury speech, July 1588

My loving people, I have always placed my chiefest strength and safeguard in the loyal hearts and good will of my subjects; and therefore I have come amongst you, being resolved, in the midst and heat of the battle, to live and die amongst you all; to lay down for my God, and for my kingdom, and my people, my honour and my blood, even in the dust. I know I have the body of a weak and feeble woman; but I have the heart and stomach of a king, and of a king of England too, and think it foul that Spain, or any prince of Europe, should dare to invade the borders of my realm! I myself will take up arms, I myself will be your general, judge, and rewarder of every one of your virtues in the field. By your valour, we shall shortly have a famous victory over those enemies of my God, of my kingdom, and of my people!

WINSTON CHURCHILL

From Churchill's speech to the House of Commons, 1940

Even though large tracts of Europe and many old and famous States have fallen or may fall into the grip of the Gestapo and all the odious apparatus of Nazi rule, we shall not flag or fail. We shall go on to the end, we shall fight in France, we shall fight on the seas and oceans, we shall fight with growing confidence and growing strength in the air, we shall defend our Island, whatever the cost may be, we shall fight on the beaches, we shall fight on the landing grounds, we shall fight in the fields and in the streets, we shall fight in the hills; we shall never surrender, and even if, which I do not for a moment believe, this Island or a large part of it were subjugated and starving, then our Empire beyond the seas, armed and guarded by the British Fleet, would carry on the struggle, until, in God's good time, the New World, with all its power and might, steps forth to the rescue and the liberation of the old.

EMMELINE PANKHURST

Adapted from a speech given in Connecticut, 1913

I am here as a soldier who has temporarily left the field of battle in order to explain what civil war is like when it is waged by women. If you are dealing with an industrial revolution, if you get the men and women of one class rising up against the men and women of another class, you can locate the difficulty. If there is a great industrial strike, you know exactly where the violence is and how the warfare is going to be waged. But in our war against the government, you can't locate it. We wear no mark; we belong to every class; we permeate every class of the community from the highest to the lowest; and so the men of my country are discovering it is absolutely impossible to stop us. In America, you won your freedom when you had the Revolution, by bloodshed, by sacrificing human life. Either women are to be killed or women are to have the vote. I ask American men in this meeting, what do you choose? There is only one answer: you must give women the vote.

ABRAHAM LINCOLN

Adapted from The House Divided, 1858 and The Gettysburg Address, 1863

Four score and seven years ago, our fathers brought forth on this continent, a new nation, conceived in Liberty, and dedicated to the proposition that all men are created equal. And yet, five years ago, I saw a house divided. I said, 'This government cannot endure, permanently, half slave and half free.' Now we are engaged in a great civil war, testing whether our nation conceived in Liberty can endure. We meet today on a great battlefield of that war. The brave men, living and dead, who struggled here, must never be forgotten. We, the living, must dedicate ourselves to their unfinished work. These dead shall not have died in vain. This nation, under God, shall have a new birth of freedom -- and that government of the people, by the people, for the people, shall not perish from the earth.

MARTIN LUTHER KING JR.

Adapted from I Have a Dream, 1963

Five score years ago, a great American, in whose symbolic shadow we stand today, signed the Emancipation Proclamation. But one hundred years later, we are still not free. I say to you today, my friends, I still have a dream. It is a dream deeply rooted in the American dream. I have a dream that one day this nation will rise up and live out the true meaning of its creed: 'We hold these truths to be self-evident; that all men are created equal.' I have a dream that one day on the red hills of Georgia, the sons of former slaves and the sons of former slave owners will be able to sit down together at the table of brotherhood. I have a dream that my four little children will one day live in a nation where they will not be judged by the colour of their skin but by the content of their character. I have a dream that one day down in Alabama, with its vicious racists, little black boys and black girls will be able to join hands with little white boys and white girls as sisters and brothers. I have a dream today. And when this happens, we will be able to join hands together and sing, 'Free at last! Free at last! Thank God Almighty, we are free at last!'

• simply •
Shakespeare

ROMEO

From Romeo & Juliet, Act II, Scene ii

But soft, what light through yonder window breaks?
It is the east and Juliet is the sun!
Arise, fair sun, and kill the envious moon,
Who is already sick and pale with grief
That thou her maid art far more fair than she.
Be not her maid, since she is envious;
Her vestal livery is but sick and green,
And none but fools do wear it. Cast it off.
It is my lady, O, it is my love!
O that she knew she were!
She speaks, yet she says nothing; what of that?
Her eye discourses, I will answer it.
I am too bold: 'tis not to me she speaks.
Two of the fairest stars in all the heaven,
Having some business, do entreat her eyes
To twinkle in their spheres till they return.
What if her eyes were there, they in her head?
The brightness of her cheek would shame those stars,
As daylight doth a lamp. Her eyes in heaven
Would through the airy region stream so bright
That birds would sing and think it were not night.
See how she leans her cheek upon her hand
O that I were a glove upon that hand,
That I might touch that cheek!

JULIET

From Romeo & Juliet, Act II, Scene ii

O Romeo, Romeo, wherefore art thou Romeo?
Deny thy father and refuse thy name.
Or if thou wilt not, be but sworn my love
And I'll no longer be a Capulet.
'Tis but thy name that is my enemy:
Thou art thyself, though not a Montague.
What's Montague? It is nor hand nor foot
Nor arm nor face nor any other part
Belonging to a man. O be some other name.
What's in a name? That which we call a rose
By any other name would smell as sweet;
So Romeo would, were he not Romeo call'd,
Retain that dear perfection which he owes
Without that title. Romeo, doff thy name,
And for that name, which is no part of thee,
Take all myself.

MACBETH

From Macbeth, Act I, Scene vii

If it were done, when 'tis done, then 'twere well
It were done quickly: if the assassination
Could trammel up the consequence, and catch
With his surcease success; that but this blow
Might be the be-all and the end-all – here,
But here, upon this bank and shoal of time,
We'd jump the life to come. But in these cases
We still have judgment here; that we but teach
Bloody instructions, which, being taught, return
To plague the inventor: this even-handed justice
Commends the ingredients of our poisoned chalice
To our own lips. He's here in double trust:
First, as I am his kinsman and his subject,
Strong both against the deed; then, as his host,
Who should against his murderer shut the door,
Not bear the knife myself. Besides, this Duncan
Hath borne his faculties so meek, hath been
So clear in his great office, that his virtues
Will plead like angels, trumpet-tongued, against
The deep damnation of his taking-off;
And pity, like a naked new-born babe,
Striding the blast, or heaven's Cherubins, hors'd
Upon the sightless couriers of the air,
Shall blow the horrid deed in every eye,
That tears shall drown the wind. I have no spur
To prick the sides of my intent, but only
Vaulting ambition, which overleaps itself
And falls on the other.

LADY MACBETH

From Macbeth, Act I, Scene v

The raven himself is hoarse,
That croaks the fatal entrance of Duncan
Under my battlements. Come, you Spirits
That tend on mortal thoughts, unsex me here,
And fill me, from the crown to the toe, top full
Of direst cruelty! Make thick my blood,
Stop up th'access and passage to remorse;
That no compunctious visitings of Nature
Shake my fell purpose, nor keep peace between
Th'effect and it! Come to my woman's breasts,
And take my milk for gall, your murth'ring ministers,
Wherever in your sightless substances,
You wait on Nature's mischief! Come, thick Night,
And pall thee in the dunnest smoke of Hell,
That my keen knife see not the wound it makes,
Nor Heaven peep through the blanket of the dark,
To cry, 'Hold, hold!'
(*Enter Macbeth*)
Great Glams! Worthy Cawdor!
Greater than both, by the all hail hereafter!
Thy letters have transported me beyond
This ignorant present, and I feel now
The future in the instant.

IAGO

From Othello, Act II, Scene iii

And what's he then that says I play the villain?
When this advice is free I give and honest,
Probal to thinking and indeed the course
To win the Moor again? For 'tis most easy
The inclining Desdemona to subdue
In any honest suit: she's framed as fruitful
As the free elements. And then for her
To win the Moor—were't to renounce his baptism,
All seals and symbols of redeemed sin,
His soul is so enfettered to her love,
That she may make, unmake, do what she list,
Even as her appetite shall play the god
With his weak function. How am I then a villain
To counsel Cassio to this parallel course,
Directly to his good? Divinity of hell!
When devils will the blackest sins put on,
They do suggest at first with heavenly shows,
As I do now: for whiles this honest fool
Plies Desdemona to repair his fortunes
And she for him pleads strongly to the Moor,
I'll pour this pestilence into his ear,
That she repeals him for her body's lust;
And by how much she strives to do him good,
She shall undo her credit with the Moor.
So will I turn her virtue into pitch,
And out of her own goodness make the net
That shall enmesh them all.

EMILIA

From Othello, Act IV, Scene iii

But I do think it is their husbands' faults
If wives do fall: say that they slack their duties,
And pour our treasures into foreign laps,
Or else break out in peevish jealousies,
Throwing restraint upon us; or say they strike us,
Or scant our former having in despite;
Why, we have galls, and though we have some grace,
Yet have we some revenge. Let husbands know
Their wives have sense like them: they see and smell
And have their palates both for sweet and sour,
As husbands have. What is it that they do
When they change us for others? Is it sport?
I think it is: and doth affection breed it?
I think it doth: is't frailty that thus errs?
It is so too: and have not we affections,
Desires for sport, and frailty, as men have?
Then let them use us well: else let them know,
The ills we do, their ills instruct us so.

CRESSIDA

From Troilus and Cressida, Act III, Scene ii

Boldness comes to me now, and brings me heart:
Prince Troilus, I have loved you night and day
For many weary months.
Hard to seem won; but I was won, my lord,
With the first glance that ever – Pardon me:
If I confess much you will play the tyrant.
I love you now, but till now not so much
But I might master it. In faith I lie –
My thoughts were like unbridled children, grown
Too headstrong for their mother. – See, we fools!
Why have I blabbed? Who shall be true to us
When we are so unsecret to ourselves? –
But though I loved you well, I wooed you not;
And yet, good faith, I wished myself a man,
Or that we women had men's privilege
Of speaking first. Sweet, bid me hold my tongue,
For in this rapture I shall surely speak
The thing I shall repent. See, see, your silence,
Cunning in dumbness, from my weak draws
My very soul of counsel. Stop my mouth.

OPHELIA

From Hamlet, Act II, Scene i

O my lord, my lord, I have been so affrighted!
My lord, as I was sewing in my closet,
Lord Hamlet, with his doublet all unbraced,
No hat upon his head, his stockings fouled,
Ungartered, and down-gyved to his ankle;
Pale as his shirt, his knees knocking each other,
And with a look so piteous in purport
As if he had been loosed out of hell
To speak of horrors- he comes before me.
He took me by the wrist and held me hard;
Then goes he to the length of all his arm,
And, with his other hand thus o'er his brow,
He falls to such perusal of my face
As he would draw it. Long stayed he so.
At last, a little shaking of mine arm,
And thrice his head thus waving up and down,
He raised a sigh so piteous and profound
As it did seem to shatter all his bulk
And end his being. That done, he lets me go,
And with his head over his shoulder turned
He seemed to find his way without his eyes,
For out o' doors he went without their help
And to the last bended their light on me.

GHOST

From Hamlet, Act I, Scene v

I am thy father's spirit,
Doomed for a certain term to walk the night,
And for the day confined to fast in fires,
Till the foul crimes done in my days of nature
Are burnt and purged away. But that I am forbid
To tell the secrets of my prison house,
I could a tale unfold whose lightest word
Would harrow up thy soul, freeze thy young blood,
Make thy two eyes, like stars, start from their spheres,
Thy knotted and combined locks to part,
And each particular hair to stand on end
Like quills upon the fretful porcupine.
But this eternal blazon must not be
To ears of flesh and blood. List, list, O, list!
If thou didst ever thy dear father love-
Revenge his foul and most unnatural murder.

HAMLET

From Hamlet, Act III, Scene i

To be, or not to be: that is the question:
Whether 'tis nobler in the mind to suffer
The slings and arrows of outrageous fortune
Or to take arms against a sea of troubles,
And by opposing end them. To die- to sleep-
No more; and by a sleep to say we end
The heartache, and the thousand natural shocks
That flesh is heir to. 'Tis a consummation
Devoutly to be wished. To die- to sleep.
To sleep- perchance to dream: ay, there's the rub!
For in that sleep of death what dreams may come
When we have shuffled off this mortal coil,
Must give us pause. There's the respect
That makes calamity of so long life.
For who would bear the whips and scorns of time,
Th' oppressor's wrong, the proud man's contumely,
The pangs of despised love, the law's delay,
The insolence of office, and the spurns
That patient merit of the unworthy takes,
When he himself might his quietus make
With a bare bodkin? Who would these fardels bear,
To grunt and sweat under a weary life,
But that the dread of something after death-
The undiscovered country, from whose bourn
No traveller returns- puzzles the will,
And makes us rather bear those ills we have
Than fly to others that we know not of?

Thus conscience does make cowards of us all,
And thus the native hue of resolution
Is sicklied o'er with the pale cast of thought,
And enterprises of great pith and moment
With this regard their currents turn awry
And lose the name of action.- Soft you now!
The fair Ophelia! Nymph, in thy orisons
Be all my sins remembered.

www.ingramcontent.com/pod-product-compliance
Ingram Content Group UK Ltd.
Pitfield, Milton Keynes, MK11 3LW, UK
UKHW020126250726
13967UKWH00002B/507

9 780648 742104